MW00622778

THE RADICAL
BOOK SHOP...
887 NORTH CLARK ST.
CHICAGO... ILLINOIS

GENERAL STRIKE

THE RADICAL BOOK SHOP OF CHICAGO

KEVIN I. SLAUGHTER

"I believe in the human intellect. I believe in demonstrating the value of my own individual type. I believe in demonstrating the value of Me to the universe. I am in search of freedom and now, at least, I am free."

—LILLIAN H. UDELL, 1915

UNION OF EGOISTS

Published April 30, 2023, by Union of Egoists
and Underworld Amusements.

www.TheRadicalBookShop.com
www.UnionOfEgoists.com
www.UnderworldAmusements.com

STAND ALONE SA1250
Paperback ISBN: 978-1-943687-28-2
Hardback ISBN: 978-1-943687-29-9

Copyediting by Daniel Acheampong.
Frontispiece illustration by Josh Latta.

Originally published as "A History of the Radical Book Shop of Chicago" in *Der Geist: A Journal of Egoism from 1845 to 1945*, Issue 3, Spring 2020. It has been revised and expanded, with new illustrations added for this edition.

Some illustrations herein courtesy of the Newberry Library of Chicago and other institutions, noted when possible.

Thank you to Daniel Acheampong for fixing an unlettered hillbilly's attempt at erudition; I marvel at your attentiveness and concision. Thank you, Jeff Bowling, for your tireless propaganda efforts, managing to sell the unsellable.

My appreciation and respect to Peter H. Gilmore, Peggy Nadramia, Mark A. Sullivan, Chip Smith, Michael Moynihan, Eric Macom, Raul Anthony, G. Johnson, Christopher R. Mealie, Daniel Byrd, Jim Goad, David Anthem, William Kelly, Carl Abrahamsson, David Sachs, Fred Woodworth, Vincent M. M. Saulsbury, Samuel Taylor, the folks at Bolerium Books, the folks at Little Black Cart, and Julie Herrada and staff of the Joseph A. Labadie Collection at the University of Michigan.

Honor to my great-grandfather Isaac S. London, who was a small newspaper publisher and wrote of local history for posterity.

Storge and *philia* to Chris X, Trevor, Ida, Norbert, Odelia, Baxter, Gwyn.

PREFACE

My telling the story of the Radical Book Shop, and the radical family who ran it, and the radical individuals who associated with it runs a bit more matter of fact than romantic. I don't consider myself a writer or historian, but nobody else has told this story that I have become so fascinated with, as Max Stirner would say, "I need your ears to hear it."

I didn't expect this to be my first book; it was first written and published as an article for the journal *Der Geist*. I then tried working it into a booklet because I had a couple of corrections to make and was so fond of it. After surpassing 50 pages, I realized it was no longer a booklet but a slim book. I have added the *accoutrement* of a "real book," such as an index and this paltry preface, but I did not go back and gratuitously pad it out for length. Much more could be written about all the names mentioned herein and the bombastic time it covers in the "city of the big shoulders" and the world events that run concurrent.

The appendix features all known writings by Lillian, the only family member I could find published work by. Since she was blind, it's fair to say the family probably had *some* role in the work. The appendix is dominated by nine items transcribed from the first (and possibly only) issue of *The Stylus*, a literary journal she edited in 1896. I was able to scan the only known extant copy, on loan from Yale University.

I have provided an index of names, titles, and locations, and I have given many sources in footnotes throughout the book.

All writers and researchers of odd old things have my gratitude, but especially my good friend and comrade Trevor Blake. The past expands before us all.

Kevin I. Slaughter
March 2023

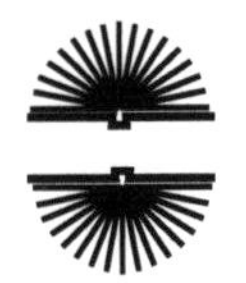

CONTENTS

APPENDIX

ANARCHIST BOOK SHOP IN CHICAGO RADICALS' MECCA

The Radical Book Shop was founded in 1914 by disillusioned social worker Howard "Harry" Lewis Udell (1870–1918) and his blind wife, Lillian Evangeline (Hiller) Udell (1867–1935), a respected lecturer on literature. Their daughters, Geraldine (1903–1998) and Phyllis (1900–1973), would assist and became integral to the running of the shop.

The "shoebox-sized" Radical Book Shop was a Chicago source for anarchist, unionist, socialist, and communist material for just over a decade. It was a place where radicals of all kinds would find inspiration and camaraderie. It became a hotspot for poets, revolutionaries, novelists, roughnecks, amateur actors, and attempted murderers of the heads of church and state. It openly sold Ragnar Redbeard's *Might is Right* alongside socialist standards and other radical works. It was one of a number of fascinating locations brimming with eccentrics, deviants, and militants. Others were Bughouse Square, Dil Pickle Club, the Gold Coast House of Corrections, Seven Arts, The House of Blazes, and the Temple of Wisdom.

While Howard died a few years in, Lillian became known as the "godmother of Chicago's hobohemia."

The egotheist Malfew Seklew was a frequenter, and it was there that Jack Jones began his weekly meetings that grew into the legendary Dil Pickle Club. One of the founders of the Industrial Workers of the World William "Bill" Haywood was often found there, holding court by the wood stove, and "Father of the Beats" Kenneth Rexroth could be seen kissing the owners' daughter on the stage in the back, one that was part of the burgeoning Little Theater movement. "Anarchist balls" were held annually, for a few years, to fundraise for the shop. Later, it became part of a co-op founded by Sherwood Anderson and his compatriots, though, eventually, it was dropped from the scheme for terminal unprofitability.

It is unclear when the Radical Book Shop finally closed its doors, but it carried on into the late '20s at least. This humble little family-run shop sent ripples through the culture that can still be felt today, however faint. While there are mentions of the store in a number of popular biographies and newspaper accounts through the years, it seems there was not one singular history. I have attempted to put together a history of the shop as it has had an impact not just on the culture of radical politics but on that of American avant-garde poetry and theater as well. It does not end in a bang, but there are at least a few explosions on the way.

Howard L. Udell was born in St. Louis on June 28th, 1870. He was ordained a Unitarian minister in 1896 and ministered to churches in Illinois, Wisconsin, and Michigan for the next eight years.

On June 30th, 1898, the printer's trade journal *The Fourth Estate* ran the following notice:

> The Kane County Journal Company, Geneva, (Ill.) has been licensed to incorporate with a capital stock of $25,000. The incorporators are Howard Udell, L.H.Udell and J.E. Forest. At the present time Rev. Udell has the money, and Mr. Forest, experience.

No more information about this printing business venture is known.

From 1905, "Harry" ran Associated Charities in a number of states, including Connecticut, Rhode Island, and Chicago. In 1908, he organized the Society for the Relief of Tuberculosis for the Associated Charities in Pawtucket.[1] In Connecticut in 1911, he advocated for juvenile courts and probation work so that "delinquent" children would not be stigmatized as criminals but instead be helped by probation officers and their families to correct the course of their lives.[2] In 1912, Mr. Udell took part in the 14th annual meeting of the American Hospital Association in Detroit, Michigan. On January 1st, 1914, Harry officially resigned from his position as Secretary of Associated Charities in Detroit.

1 *The Survey: Social, Charitable, Civic: A Journal of Constructive Philanthropy*. December 18, 1909.

2 "Probation", *The Survey*, March 18, 1911.

▲ Cover of *What is to be done? Life* by Lyof N. Tolsoi (Thomas Y. Crowell Co., New York, 1899) (reduced) with overset book trade label from the Radical Book Shop (enlarged), scanned from the title page.

Mr. Udell was described as "absolutely broken in health" by assistant secretary Mary Hubert:

> Mr. Udell will never admit his health is broken, but those who have watched him for the last three months know that the long hours, the tremendous number of investigations and reports which have come under his supervision, have told upon his health and have made it necessary for him to resign.[3]

Another source tells a different story, though, one in which Howard was so frustrated with how poorly social services and other organizations helped the poor and working classes, he quit in disgust to explore more radical ideas.

Lillian, born in Dunkirk, N.Y., was a women's rights activist and lecturer in literature. There are notices of her speaking on "Feminism in Literature",[4] Irish Poetry, and Ibsen. The Freeport, Illinois, *Daily Journal* on Feb. 8th, 1897, in reporting a forthcoming lecture of hers on "Our Literary Idols" at the Globe Hall, quotes the *Kalamazoo News*:

> Mrs. Udell brings that rare combination of sympathy and critical judgment which enables one to get the best from such an author without blindly worshiping his faults and eccentricities.
>
> Her fine and accurate knowledge of general literature and familiarity with marked phrases of thoughts, past and present, were made apparent in the course of an address that was classic in every sentence, though delivered very simply with no

3 "H.L. Udell Quits; Broken in Health", *Detroit Free Press*, Nov. 18th, 1913.

4 "Announcements", *The Day Book*, July 10th, 1916.

> attempt at oratorical effect. Mrs. Udell is a scholar and a thinker who deserves and will win the appreciation of those who care for both common and uncommon sense in dealing with the great questions and great writers of the day.
>
> The unusual culture of her mind is the more remarkable that it has been gained under the profound disability of total blindness since the second year of her age. In presence she is graceful and gracious, and voice, language and thought all betoken extreme refinement and sensitiveness of soul.

The *Freeport Daily Democrat* then followed up with a long write-up about the lecture,[5] which has been reproduced in full as an appendix. In it, and other write-ups of stops on this speaking tour, it is mentioned that Lillian was the editor of *The Stylus*. The tour was certainly done to promote the journal.[6]

Lillian was blind since her childhood, though some stories (most certainly wrong) claim it happened later in life. In 1889, "Mrs. H.L. Udell" of Michigan was listed as being indebted to, among many other women, the American Women Suffrage Association for "State reports." In 1891, "Mrs. H.L. Udell" was listed as a "local committee" in the souvenir book for the 19th Congress of the Association for the Advancement of Women that took place in Grand Rapids, MI. She attended the Meadville Theological Seminary[7] but

5 *Freeport Daily Democrat*, Feb. 12th, 1897.

6 Shortly before publication, I was able to secure the only known copy from Yale University's Library. All of Lillian's writings from the issue have been transcribed and included in the Appendix.

7 *The Unitarian: A Monthly Magazine of Liberal Christianity*, Vol. 9 No. 12, December 1894.

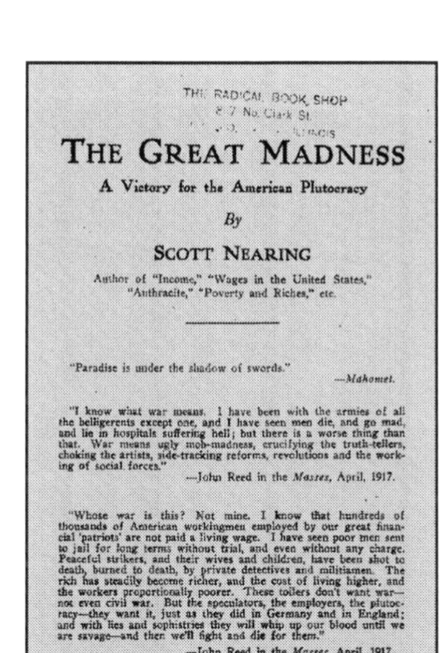

THE RADICAL BOOK SHOP
867 No. Clark St.
ILLINOIS

THE GREAT MADNESS

A Victory for the American Plutocracy

By

SCOTT NEARING

Author of "Income," "Wages in the United States," "Anthracite," "Poverty and Riches," etc.

"Paradise is under the shadow of swords."
—*Mahomet.*

"I know what war means. I have been with the armies of all the belligerents except one, and I have seen men die, and go mad, and lie in hospitals suffering hell; but there is a worse thing than that. War means ugly mob-madness, crucifying the truth-tellers, choking the artists, side-tracking reforms, revolutions and the working of social forces."
—John Reed in the *Masses*, April, 1917.

"Whose war is this? Not mine. I know that hundreds of thousands of American workingmen employed by our great financial 'patriots' are not paid a living wage. I have seen poor men sent to jail for long terms without trial, and even without any charge. Peaceful strikers, and their wives and children, have been shot to death, burned to death, by private detectives and militiamen. The rich has steadily become richer, and the cost of living higher, and the workers proportionally poorer. These toilers don't want war—not even civil war. But the speculators, the employers, the plutocracy—they want it, just as they did in Germany and in England; and with lies and sophistries they will whip up our blood until we are savage—and then we'll fight and die for them."
—John Reed in the *Masses*, April, 1917.

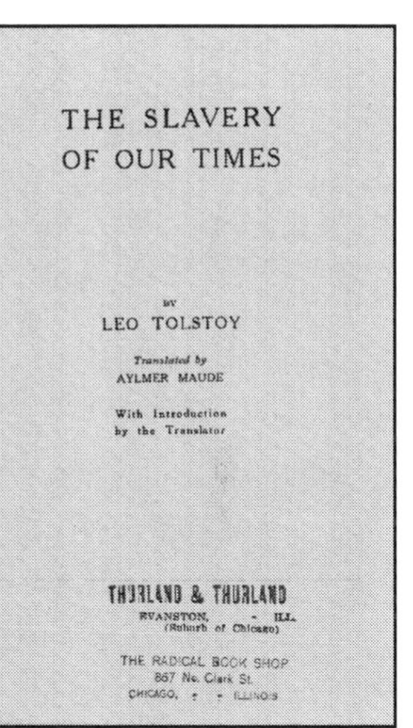

THE SLAVERY OF OUR TIMES

BY

LEO TOLSTOY

Translated by
AYLMER MAUDE

With Introduction
by the Translator

THURLAND & THURLAND
EVANSTON, - ILL.
(Suburb of Chicago)

THE RADICAL BOOK SHOP
867 No. Clark St.
CHICAGO, - - ILLINOIS

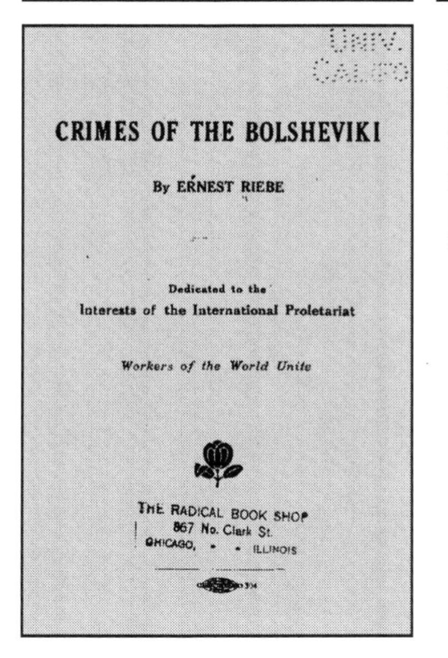

CRIMES OF THE BOLSHEVIKI

By ERNEST RIEBE

Dedicated to the
Interests of the International Proletariat

Workers of the World Unite

THE RADICAL BOOK SHOP
867 No. Clark St.
CHICAGO, - - ILLINOIS

◂ Title pages to three books ink-stamped by the Radical Book Shop to mark the passage through their store. Tolstoy's *The Slavery of Our Times* was additionally stamped by Arthur Desmond as being sold through his Thurland and Thurland book shop and publishing house.

left without graduating in 1893.

It's unclear when Harry and Lillian were married, but the first appearance of Lillian as a writer is an essay in Benjamin R. Tucker's anarchist journal *Liberty*. On the topic of Ibsen from Vol. 11, No. 4 (Whole No. 316), June 29th, 1895, it was signed "Mrs. Howard Udell".[8]

8 Along with others, this essay has been transcribed and included as anappendix.

▲ This portrait of Harry L. Udell is from the *Detroit Free Press*, Nov. 18th, 1913. Unfortunately, no pictures of Lillian have been discovered.

FROM SIDEWALK TO SHOEBOX, A STORE IS BORN

The bookstore was a hub for radical literature,[9] sold tickets to Emma Goldman lectures, and even became part of the burgeoning "little theater" movement. Beginning at 954 N. Clark Street, it was just around the corner from the Oak Hall that served as a meeting place for "Wobblies" and where they would hold fundraising dances in the early days. There was great overlap between the frequenters of the Radical Book Shop and the Dil Pickle Club.[10] Through Howard Udell's membership, the store had close ties to the Industrial Workers of the World, founded in Chicago in 1905. The "Wobblies" were social revolutionaries who advocated the replacement of capitalism with "industrial democracy" and did so through organizing workers and going on strike.

One of the habitués of the Radical Book Shop was egoist author Malfew Seklew, who is said to have gone there to read the dictionary to expand his already verbose vocabulary. Also purported to frequent the shop was artist Stanisław Szukalski. The Polish visionary had a studio nearby and was in Chicago from 1913 until the mid-'20s. The Joe Hill

---

9 One such journal was *The Messenger*, founded in 1917, in New York City, by Chandler Owen and A. Philip Randolph; it was a journal integral to the growth of the Harlem Renaissance.

10 The Dil Pickle Club was frequented by such notable figures as author Ben Hecht, artist Stanisław Szukalski (who had a studio next door), egotheist Sirfessor Wilkesbarre (*aka* Malfew Seklew), Carl Sandburg, and the "whorehouse doctor" Ben Reitman. Mae West, Clarence Darrow, Mary MacLane, Magnus Hirschfeld, and Max Bodenheim all spoke or performed there. The Dil Pickle Press published the 1927 edition of *Might is Right* by Ragnar Redbeard, the last edition published in the author's lifetime. Franklin Rosemont's book *The Rise & Fall of the Dil Pickle Club* (Chicago: Charles H. Kerr, 2013) is highly recommended.

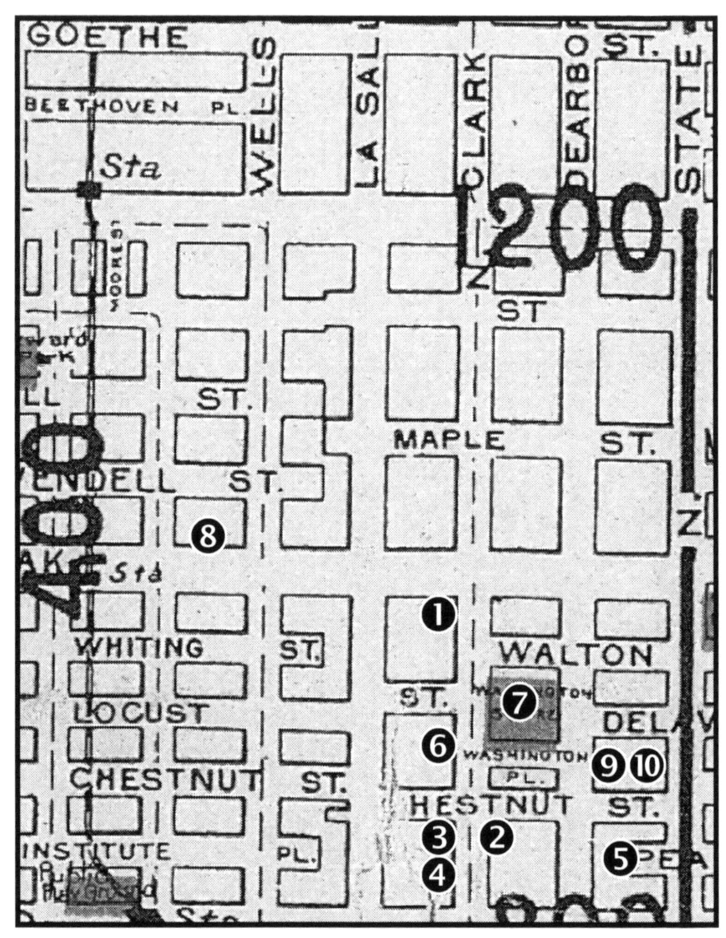

❶—954 N. Clark St., first location of the Radical Book Shop.
❷ —817½ N. Clark St., second location of the Radical Book Shop.
❸—826 N. Clark St., Turner Hall, third location of the Radical Book Shop.
❹—832 N. Clark St., fourth address of the Radical Book Shop. Still at Turner Hall, and 826 would still be used.
❺—19 W. Pearson St., 1916 location of the Dil Pickle Club. Lillian lectured at this location many times.
❻—857 N. Clark St., Geo. Engelke, Bookseller. Associate of Arthur Desmond and seller of *Might is Right*.
❼—Washington Square Park, a.k.a. Bughouse Square.
❽—220 W. Oak St., Baker's Hall.
❾—Tooker Alley, later main location of the Dil Pickle Club.
❿—Studio of visionary Polish artist Stanisław Szukalski. Right next to the Dil Pickle Club, where he lectured.

biography[11] details other names of note that sought out comradeship at the shop: Vincent St. John, Lucy Parsons, Jim Larkin, Carl Sandburg, Edgar Lee Masters, and others.

The June 1914 issue of Charles H. Kerr's *International Socialist Review* contained the following notice:

> **A Radical Book Shop.**—For a long time a perception has been growing among thinking people that Chicago needed headquarters for all radical literature. Such a shop has been opened at 954 North Clark street. Send in your orders for any book you want and when in the city don't fail to call. Lowest prices on all books pertaining to free thought in religion, science, economics, feminism and all departments of sociology. Address all correspondence to Radical Book Shop, 954 North Clark Street, Chicago.

And while the *International Socialist Review* gives its story of the creation of this interesting little place that has had a lasting impact on the arts and politics, an April 2nd, 1916, article in the *Chicago Tribune* tells a different, less idealistic story. As part of Fanny Butcher's "Tabloid Book Review" column in the Sunday edition, she said,

> A couple of years ago (Howard and Lillian Udell) were actually in want. To keep from starving they took the books from their unusual library, spread them out on some boards across an alley in North Clark street, and for two days they held their little street shop. Passersby stopped at the unusual sight, and stopped

11 Franklin Rosemont, *Joe Hill: The IWW & The Making of a Revolutionary Workingclass Culture* (Oakland: PM Press, 2015).

longer when they read the titles of the books for sale.

Then a man came along, a man who owned a cubby hole of a shop near the alley. "You can't have a shop here," he said, meaning the alley, "but you can here," meaning the cubby hole. They moved into the little twelve foot place. Mr. Udell put up book shelves. Friends of his I.W.W. workers, eager young anarchists every one, turned in and helped. Books that couldn't be found in the élite book shops were to be had there.

Illustrator and poet Ralph Chaplin tells his own version:[12]

> Charles Kerr had a friend, a former minister of the Gospel, who had turned rationalist. His name was Udell. He and his wife, a blind, highly cultured lady, were philosophical anarchists. They had two daughters, Geraldine and Phyllis. Kerr had set them all up in business at 817½ North Clark Street in what subsequently became the landmark known as the Radical Book Shop.

Around this time, the Radical Book Shop was placing half- and full-page ads in Chicago's arts journal *The Little Review,* edited by Margaret C. Anderson.[13] That journal was

---

12 *The Rise & Fall of the Dil Pickle Club* (Chicago: Charles H. Kerr, 2013). The involvement of Kerr in the opening of the shop seems to originate with Chaplin's book. I cannot find any contemporary corroboration, nor does Allen Ruff make any connection at all to the shop and the Udells in his book *We Called Each Other Comrade: Charles H. Kerr & Company, Radical Publishers* (Oakland: PM Press, 2011).

13 *The Little Review* was a staple journal at the Radical Book Shop, along with *The Arts, Others,* and many other literary journals.

the American "sister" of *The Egoist,*[14] a journal Dora Marsden founded and wrote for.

The first and best description of their second location comes from a love story serialized in the *Chicago Tribune* in 1915. The series was titled "The Love Letters of a Lonely Girl," and finding a passing reference to the bookshop is delightfully incongruous for a story that begins, "Big Dear You: Here is Little Me for a talk with you again." From the third installment (April 4th), I excerpt the pertinent section:

> En route homeward my eye caught a curious sign—an unpretentious board with "Radical Book Shop," in small letters, and beneath, in large letters, "Laundry," upon it. I stopped before the tiny window. Through it, beyond the books displayed, of Marx, Nietzsche, Tolstoy, and Breiux, I saw a tall pallid man reading to a woman. Her back was to the window. Curiosity impelled me in. What were they reading?
>
> "That's fine, dear," I heard her say as I closed the door on entering. Not more than two people could stand side by side within the shop, it was so small. There were perhaps half a hundred books on the shelves; they were fierce, bristley looking sort of books—I didn't recognize them, even by name, except Tolstoy and Brieux. Half ashamed of my curiosity—for this place did not seem a shop to prowl about in, somehow—I stammered out that I wanted *The House of Pomegranates*. The woman arose and came forward

14 Ezra Pound was a onetime literary editor of *The Egoist*, a foreign correspondent for *Poetry* magazine, and, in 1917, became foreign editor of *The Little Review*, though he still contributed articles to the prior. "In so far as it is possible, I should like *The Little Review* to aid and abet *The Egoist* in its work," Pound wrote in the editorial of the May 1917 issue.

RADICAL BOOK SHOP

Headquarters for the sale of radical literature representing all phases of libertarian thought in religion, economics, philosophy, also revolutionary fiction, poetry and drama. All current radical newspapers and magazines.

Mail orders promptly filled. Send for catalogue.

$817\frac{1}{2}$ North Clark Street

Chicago, Illinois

▲ Full-page advertisement for the Radical Book Shop from *The Little Review*, Vol. II, No. 4, June–July 1915.

gropingly. Then I saw—she was blind! No, they did not have it; they carried only radical books.

I was humbled and awed before her. The little shop had suddenly become a sanctuary.

There was a sizable write-up on the bookstore in the *Chicago Tribune* of May 11th, 1915, noting that half the "tiny box of a room" was the book shop, the other half was a "3 cent lunch," and the sign out front advertised their hand-laundry services. The article listed the types of reformers and revolutionaries that would gather around the stove in the back of the shop: socialists, single-taxers, philosophical anarchists, syndicalists, New Thoughters, Industrial Workers of the World, Bearers of the Cosmic Light, rationalists, Christian socialists, and futurists. The lighthearted story gives an anecdote under the subheading "Anarchist No More":

> During the noon hour, while Mr. and Mrs. Udell were at luncheon, the shop was left in charge of their two small daughters. And it may surprise the parents to learn that their eldest, a pretty child of 14, has recently deserted her inherited belief in philosophical anarchy.
>
> "I used to be an anarchist," she said, "but I am not any longer. I changed just a few weeks ago. Somebody stole the rugs we put in our front hall, so that things would look a little nicer. And lots and lots of times somebody steals our bottles of milk. Of course I know the theory that they need the things more than we do. Perhaps they were hungry and did need the milk, but I don't see why they needed to take our rugs."

Another *Tribune* article from 1917 gave a further description: "The shop is about six feet wide and runs back twenty-eight or thirty feet. A bit of a two foot counter holds a cash register in front."

On October 25th, the Radical Book Store made it to the "Society and Entertainment" column when socialite Virginia Pope[15] stepped into the store:

> That society maids do interest themselves in other things than dancing, bridge, and tea parties was proven again last week when Miss Virginia Pope, daughter of Mrs. Francis Pope of 62 East Oak street, wandered into the Radical Book Shop, that unique bit of radical space at 817 North Clark street... and inquired into the principles of the place where gather many interesting people for interesting discussion.
>
> So interested did she become in the attitude of ideas that she found there and in the two little girls, Phyllis and Geraldine, that she suggested afternoon teas where many of her fashionable friends would be eager to come and learn of the facts and fancies of the labor world.
>
> Miss Pope has interested herself in equal suffrage for some time and is an active member of the association of that name, and no doubt will find much to be enthusiastic about in the activities that are discussed at the Radical Bookshop, should her plan materialize.

15 Virginia Pope moved to New York and joined the *New York Times* in 1925, where she would become fashion editor. A fashion designer named Pauline Trigere was quoted in Miss Pope's 1978 obituary: "I think she invented the reporting of fashion."

Here's a fine chance
To have a good dance,
Bring friend and bring neighbor,
Bring comrades in labor,
Bring good fellows all
To the Radical ball.[16]

The Day Book[17] newspaper of May 20th, 1915, mentioned the "friends of the Radical Book Shop" were organizing a dance to be held at Baker's Hall (220 W. Oak St.) that Friday and tickets were 25 cents. This may have been the first of a series of similar events.

On April 6th, 1916, the same paper featured an article titled "Expect a Big Time at the Radical Book Shop Ball."

> Socialists, single taxers, anarchists, I. W. W.'s, university settlement workers and birth controllers are all backing the Radical Book Shop ball Friday night in Oak Hall, 220 W. Oak st.
>
> Bill Haywood and Elizabeth Gurley Flynn will lead the grand march. Rev. Wm. Thurston Brown will give out programs. Henry M. Hyde, social

16 This poem leads an item about the Radical Book Shop Ball from the *Chicago Tribune* (Chicago, Illinois) of April 2nd, 1916, pg. 66.

17 *The Day Book* was an advertising-free daily newspaper. It was available for sale at the Radical Book Shop. Ralph Chaplin, in his book *Wobbly: The Rough-and-Tumble Story of an American Radical*, recalled Carl Sandburg dropping in for news items for the paper. Letters from *The Day Book* are featured in a significant part of *The Gospel According to Malfew Seklew* (Baltimore: Underworld Amusements, 2014), and the paper also ran the *The Outbursts of Everett True* comics, later compiled into a book by Underworld Amusements (2015).

> justice editor of the *Tribune*, and Wm. L. Chenery, editor of "The Guide Post" in the *Herald*, will be there with bells on.
>
> "Every community ought to have a book store like the Radical Book Shop," said Edgar Lee Masters. "I like to step in there and see shelves of books sometimes called dangerous, but representing all shades of rebellion and protest. The shop is unique and its ball should be patronized. I don't agree with nine-tenths of its books, but I can see a healthy ferment from it."

After some background information (already covered), it continues,

> Sometimes a real mixed crowd is caught in the hang-out. One afternoon, for instance, were standing around looking at books and talking, these:
>
> Jim Larkin, famous strike leader from Ireland; Edna Kenton, writer for the *Saturday Evening Post*, the *Bookman* and other magazines, also the author of one novel that was a "best seller"; two members of the I. W. W. national executive board from out of town; Fannie Butcher, special writer for the *Tribune*; Harry Herwitz, secretary to Ald. Merriam; three charity workers; Rev. J. C. Ashurst, a Baptist minister; Leslie H. Marcey, editor *International Socialist Review*; Margaret Merriman, actress with Chester Wallace Players, and stage people from the *So Long Letty*, *The Weavers* and the Little Theater companies.
>
> It is a sort of clearing house and news center for the radical world. The shop hasn't reached the point

> where it pays a living wage profit to the Udells. So its friends want to see a big crowd at the ball Friday night.

On November 16th, 1916, there was a notice that a dance was being held at "Oak Hall" again, but no other notices have been found.

Ralph Chaplin, in his recollections,[18] discusses some of the characters who made up the milieu of the Radical Book Shop:

> It was there that Bill Haywood, during his first year in Chicago, used to spend evenings with a small group of friends and kindred spirits around an old round-bellied stove back of the book counter in the rear of the store. Jim Larkin came here to meet Bill for interminable arguments about class-struggle philosophy and strategy. Carl Sandburg would drop in now and then for bits of labor news for the *Day Book*. He

18 *Wobbly: The Rough-and-Tumble Story of an American Radical* (Chicago: Univ. of Chicago Press, 1948).

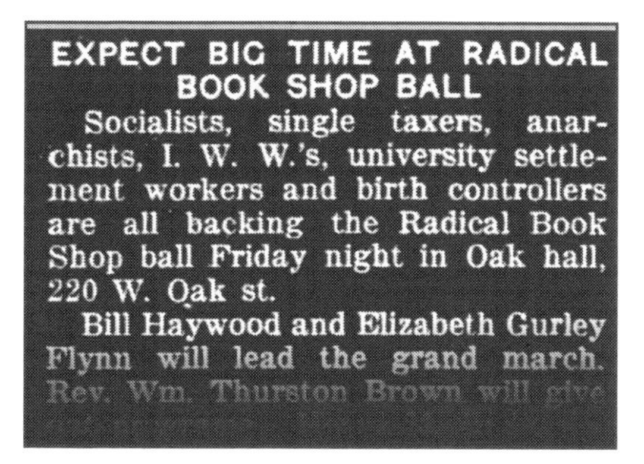

EXPECT BIG TIME AT RADICAL BOOK SHOP BALL

Socialists, single taxers, anarchists, I. W. W.'s, university settlement workers and birth controllers are all backing the Radical Book Shop ball Friday night in Oak hall, 220 W. Oak st.

Bill Haywood and Elizabeth Gurley Flynn will lead the grand march. Rev. Wm. Thurston Brown will give

▲ Announcement from *The Day Book* of April 6th, 1916.

was a stranger to most of us at the time, having only recently moved to Chicago from Milwaukee, where he had worked on Victor Berger's *Socialist Leader*. The Radical Book Shop was a hangout for radicals of all shades of red and black, as well as for the Near North Side intelligentsia. Bill didn't get on so well with the latter element. Ben Reitman he detested as he did Jack Jones. Jack was at that time working for the A.F. of L. Painters' Union. Between chores for this union Jack was establishing his famous "Dil Pickle Club" in the alley called Tooker Court. Bill could never forgive him for his stand on decentralization at the 1912 I.W.W. convention.

The bohemian crowd that frequented the Radical Book Shop was dominated by the overwhelming personality of a young Swedish poet of local fame, J. J. Florine.[19] Several local newspaper reporters, and very minor poets like myself, paid him occasional mock homage as "Om"—High Factotum of the "Bearers of the Cosmic Light." Once in a while, we would foregather at a nearby saloon, drink beer, and recite poems, satirical or otherwise. Florine was cynical, disillusioned, and smart. "Death, Destruction, and Decay," he proclaimed, "represent the universal lifecycle. Why get excited about it?" One round of beer a week was the cost of membership. As long as there were only five of us, I did quite well. But the "Bearers of the Cosmic Light" increased rapidly—too rapidly for me. The pay-off came one night when we were all kicked out of a saloon because we held an Omar Khayyâm session on election day. I got the worst of it

19 In documents from the period, his name is written "G.G. Florine."

that time because I happened to be the largest man in the group. Every hoodlum on North Clark Street, it seemed, landed his fist somewhere on my person. Bill Haywood was delighted when he surveyed my black eyes and swollen cheekbones and chin. He didn't like Near North Side bohemians and was always warning me against them. Bill hadn't taken a drink since his arrival in Chicago.

The Naked Truth of Jesusism

From Oriental Manuscripts in the light of Modern Criticism. By LYMAN F. GEORGE. Dedicated to the Daring Dreamers. Just published, cloth, 60c postpaid. Book catalog FREE. Address

Radical Book Shop

817½ North Clark Street, Chicago

▲ Advertisement from *International Socialist Review*, Vol. XV, No.9, March 1915. The book advertised is *The Naked Truth of Jesusism from Oriental Manuscripts*, by Lyman Fairbanks George (Pittsburgh: The George Book Pub. Co., 1914). This author was surprised to discover it is a "rhythmical protest in fourteen cantos."

What is the Revolutionists' attitude towards LOVE AND MARRIAGE?

Here is one man's answer to this question sincerely and eloquently expressed—

The Evolution of Sexual Morality, By Wm. Thurston Brown, 10 Cents
Love's Freedom and Fulfillment " " " " 10 Cents
The Moral Basis of the Demand for Free Divorce " " 10 Cents

These three pamphlets sent postpaid upon receipt of 25 Cents

RADICAL BOOK SHOP

817½ No. Clark St. CHICAGO, ILL.

▲ Advertisement from *International Socialist Review*, Vol. 15, No.5, November 1914. The magazine was edited and published by Charles H. Kerr. Issues also advertised and sold the infamous Chicago book *Might is Right* by Ragnar Redbeard.

POISONING THE GOVERNOR, THE MAYOR, AND THE ARCHBISHOP

A reporter visited Bill Haywood on Feb 12th, 1916, while he was at the Radical Book Shop. Haywood was among a group of Wobblies who were reading news articles about Jean Crones, an anarchist who worked as a cook while catering for a large party. Crones attempted to murder several hundred of Chicago's most influential politicians, businessmen, and even the archbishop.

While initially it was thought that Crones was a German agent, it was discovered he was an Italian anarchist named Nestor Dondoglio. Nestor was part of the Luigi Galleani circle of insurrectionary anarchists, known for their "propaganda of the deed." Galleani published a journal titled *Cronaca Sovversiva* (*Subversive Chronicle*), and it was said of him, "You heard Galleani speak, and you were ready to shoot the first policeman you saw".[20]

Mark Jacob, in the *Chicago Tribune*, noted,

> Illinois Gov. Edward Dunne was there, along with former Gov. Charles Deneen, former Chicago Mayor Carter Harrison Jr., utility czar Samuel Insull, bishops, bank presidents, judges and the superintendent of schools.

But while many got very sick, nobody actually died. There are slightly conflicting stories as to why this is. The one constant is that Dondoglio poured arsenic into the soup, but why it became diluted is up in the air. One source has

20 Avrich, Paul, *Anarchist Voices: An Oral History of Anarchism in America* (Princeton: Princeton University Press, 1996).

it that due to an additional 50 guests being added to the party, the soup was diluted, while another says that a different cook thought the broth had spoiled on taste-testing and replaced most of it with new, unpoisoned stock.

"All I know is what I read in the newspapers", Haywood is reported to have said, in denial of knowing anything about the crime or the man who perpetrated it. He denied that the man was a member of his organization. The I.W.W. members that were hanging out with Bill Haywood at the Radical Book Shop had a different theory: "It was a setup by the cops."

Dondoglio was never caught and died peacefully in Connecticut in 1932.

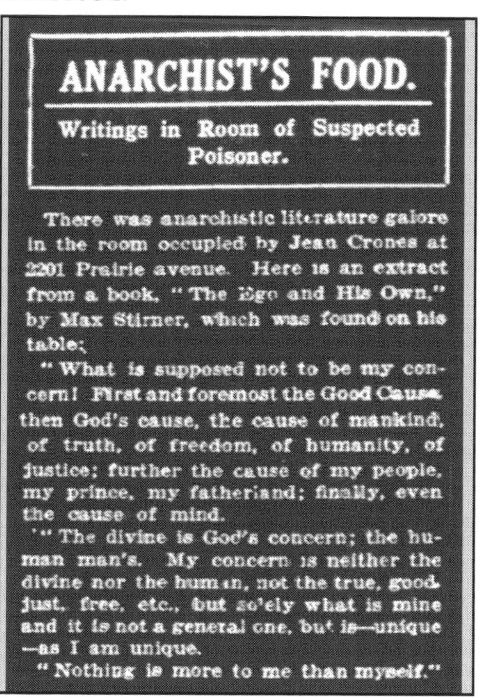

ANARCHIST'S FOOD.

Writings in Room of Suspected Poisoner.

There was anarchistic literature galore in the room occupied by Jean Crones at 2201 Prairie avenue. Here is an extract from a book, "The Ego and His Own," by Max Stirner, which was found on his table:

"What is supposed not to be my concern! First and foremost the Good Cause, then God's cause, the cause of mankind, of truth, of freedom, of humanity, of justice; further the cause of my people, my prince, my fatherland; finally, even the cause of mind.

'"The divine is God's concern; the human man's. My concern is neither the divine nor the human, not the true, good, just, free, etc., but solely what is mine and it is not a general one, but is—unique—as I am unique.

"Nothing is more to me than myself."

▲ "Anarchist's Food" reads the leader above a story from the *Chicago Tribune* (Chicago, Illinois) of Feb. 13th, 1916. Of note is the edited excerpt from the preamble of *The Ego and His Own* by Max Stirner, translated by Steven T. Byington and published by Benjamin R. Tucker.

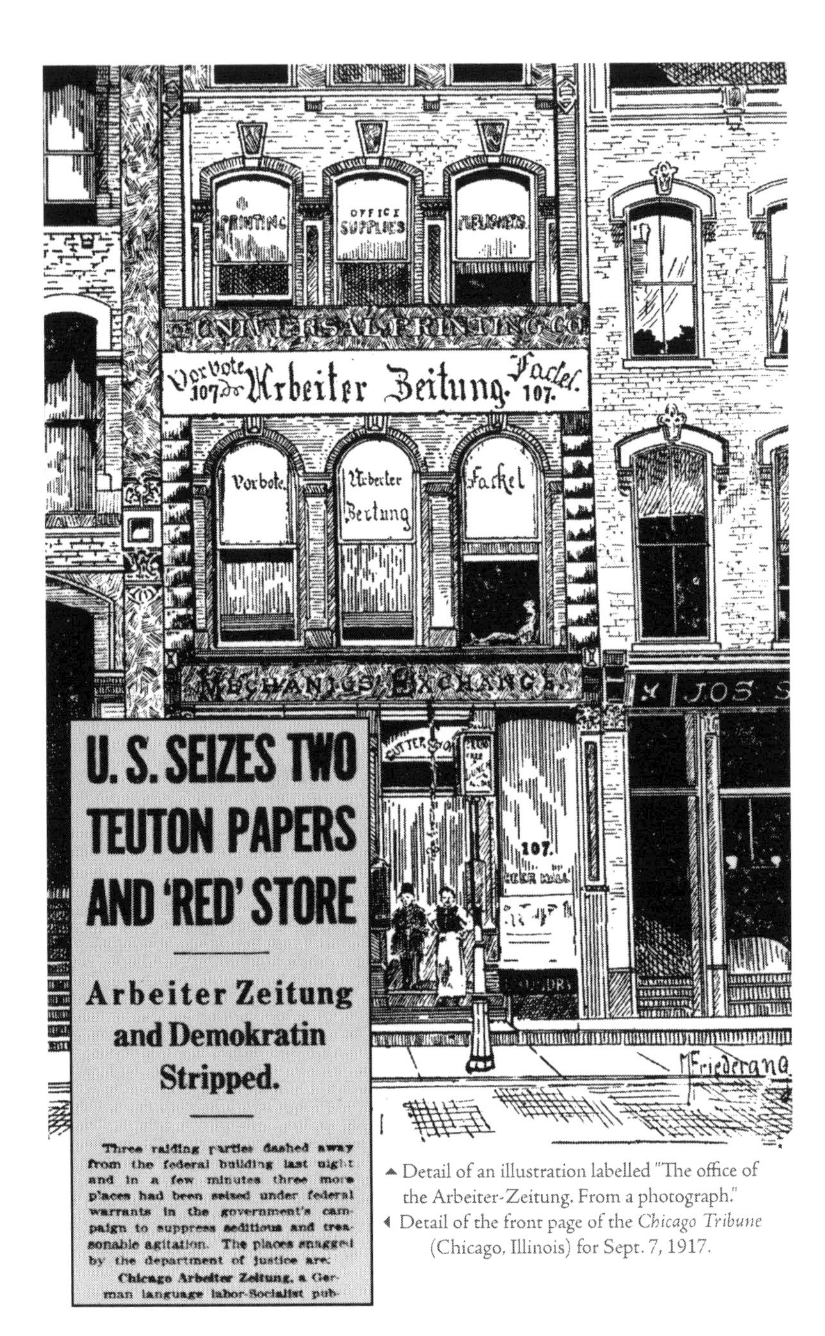

U. S. SEIZES TWO TEUTON PAPERS AND 'RED' STORE

Arbeiter Zeitung and Demokratin Stripped.

Three raiding parties dashed away from the federal building last night and in a few minutes three more places had been seized under federal warrants in the government's campaign to suppress seditious and treasonable agitation. The places snagged by the department of justice are:

Chicago Arbeiter Zeitung, a German language labor-Socialist pub-

▲ Detail of an illustration labelled "The office of the Arbeiter-Zeitung. From a photograph."

◀ Detail of the front page of the *Chicago Tribune* (Chicago, Illinois) for Sept. 7, 1917.

September 5th, 1917, saw the federal government raid I.W.W. halls and offices across the country, arresting 165 members, 100 of whom would be found guilty "of more than 10,000 individual violations of federal law" in an ensuing Chicago trial. Theron P. Cooper was one of the leaders of the Industrial Workers of the World who were charged with conspiracy to obstruct the war in 1918. *Clarence Darrow: Attorney for the Damned* by John A. Farrell, a biography of the famed attorney, merely refers to Cooper as "a pacifist."

The next day, more warrants were issued, but this time for two German-language newspapers and the Radical Book Shop. An article published in the *Chicago Tribune* under the title "U.S. Seizes Two Teuton Papers and 'Red' Store" gave detail:

> Three raiding parties dashed away from the federal building last night and in a few minutes three more places had been seized under federal warrants in the government's campaign to suppress seditious and treasonable agitation. The places snagged by the department of justice are:
>
> **Chicago Arbeiter Zeitung**, a German language labor-Socialist publication, 1642 North Halstead street, nicknamed "The Flaming Torch".
>
> **The Social Demokraten**, a German language Socialist newspaper, 2003 North California avenue, said to have been very outspoken.[21]

21 Both of these papers were sold at the Radical Book Shop.

The Radical Book Store, 817 1/2 North Clark street, where radical publications of many kinds are sold; long under surveillance.

BOLD IN CRITICISM.

These places were seized under warrants issued by Judge Evan Evans, identical with the eight he issued the day before the I.W.W. and other raids. The two German language newspapers, the federal officials say, have grown bold in their criticisms of the government.

The Radical Book store has been a sort of rendezvous for disgruntled individuals and the jobless who have come there to purchase radical books and pamphlets. There and in nearby saloons they have talked over their woes. The habitues of the immediate district have been "checked up" by the officials for two or three years back.

After some retelling of the raids on the newspapers, the story focuses on the bookstore:

STORE STRIPPED.

When a reporter visited the Radical Book Shop a few minutes after the raid he found Harry L. Udell, its keeper, and his blind wife, in the dingy little shop where for years they have earned a livelihood by selling radical and anarchistic literature. The shop is about six feet wide and runs back twenty-eight or thirty feet. A bit of a two foot counter holds a cash register in front. Udell and his wife declined to talk. But the walls of the obscure little place told the story mutely. An hour before socialistic and I.W.W. literature had lined the interior. Now there were blank places whence the "goods" had been torn.

The operatives evidently knew what they wanted: had the books and pamphlets they were to take spotted. They came in, worked swiftly, and were gone almost before the neighborhood knew they were there. No resistance was offered.

BITTER FOOD FOR THOUGHT.

Mrs. Udell, blind for years, had listened to the chatter of those who came to the shop for so long that she is known as a strong Socialist locally. She has visited around in the neighborhood and has spoken her mind freely. With the rest of the world shut out the little woman has sat in darkness and has had for a long time as her chief mental nourishment the embittered thoughts of agitators who knew the shop as their rendezvous.

The neighborhood used to be largely inhabited by Socialists who aired their views from curbs at night. Close by, at Chicago avenue and Clark street, above the saloon of "Spike" Hennessy, is a hall where the Socialist clan used to gather.

Down at Oak Street and Franklin is a Baker's Hall, also a rendezvous for a long time for Socialists and I.W.W. fanatics. In these places and in this neighborhood the police have been called many times and have dispersed many a rioting crowd.

ANTI-WAR CLANS BOOM TRADE.

Such was the neighborhood that used, in time gone

> by, to give the Radical Book Shop its bit of prosperity. Then for a long time it did not do so well. More recently anti-war agitators, pacifists, and pro-German propaganda spreaders have been active and business began to return.
>
> In a way the sooty little book store, picturesque in itself, is said to be a sort of "official canteen" for the clans who gathered there after their own ways and to speak their own thoughts.

In December of that year, the *Chicago Tribune*[22] noted a three-hour meeting of "One hundred and ten self-pronounced I.W.W.'s who, according to one of them, 'may or may not be of service to the government in the war.'" They met in King's Restaurant, and some of the members under indictment spoke:

> Then Mrs. Udell, exhaling the smoke from a cigaret, rose and praised the speakers.
>
> "I cannot help but believe that a revolution such as took place in Russia is about to occur in the United States," she said.

22 *Chicago Tribune*, Friday, December 14th, 1917

DEATH OF A FOUNDER AND A NEW LIFE

In 1918, Harry Udell died, leaving his wife and children destitute. The store never made money, and though Lillian was well known as a passionate, capable, and intellectual woman, she was blind and had two girls to take care of.

The "Chicago Co-Operative Bookstores Company" was founded by novelist Sherwood Anderson[23] (who also frequented the Dil Pickle Club). I.W.W. activist and Harvard Alumni Theron P. Cooper issued shares for the store before moving it to 826 N. Clark St. Some stories falsely state that 1918 was the year the Radical Book Store was *opened*, but it was really a continuation "under new ownership."

A short piece written in 1919 by Guido Bruno[24] highlights the connection between the bookstore and the Dil Pickle Club[25]:

> The Radical Book Shop is right around the corner. It is a co-operative store with a large stock of ultra-radical pamphlets and magazines, the meeting place for all sorts of Bolsheviki, pleasant Bolsheviki, who want to intoxicate themselves with words rather than with deeds, who are more eager to have a

23 According to *Sherwood Anderson's Secret Love Letters*, edited by Ray Lewis White (Baton Rouge: Louisiana State University Press, 1991), it was in 1920 that the Radical Book Shop hosted one of two known exhibits of the paintings of Sherwood Anderson.

24 Published in *Adventures in American Bookshops, Antique Stores and Auction Rooms* by Guido Bruno, (Detroit : The Douglas Book Shop, 1922).

25 There is no "correct" way to write the name of Jack Jones' club. Dil Pickle, Dill Pickle, or Dillpickle are all more or less correct, as seen on posters and promotional material from the club itself.

LILLIAN HILLER UDELL TO SPEAK IN DAVENPORT

The Davenport Philosophical society has secured Lillian Hiller Udell to give seven lectures in Davenport, beginning at 2:30 o'clock next Sunday afternoon at the Knights of Pythias hall, 104 West Second street. They will be given every Sunday afternoon.

Lillian Hiller Udell is an unrecognized Helen Keller. Losing her sight at the age of two years, she has compensated her loss by an intellectual development that is an inspiration, and her interpretation of Russian literature is the work of an artist.

The subject will be delivered in the following order:

"Dostieffsky and the Russian Soul."

"Turgenieff and Nihilism."

"Tolstoy, The Christian Anarchist."

"Tchekoff and Russian Pessimism."

"Gorkey, The Voice of the Worker."

"Andreyv and the Spirit of Revolt."

"Artzibashef, The Passing of the Old Order."

▲ Announcement from *Quad-City Times* (Davenport, Iowa), March 12th, 1920.

good time under present conditions than to be martyrs for a new and better world. And when they want to amuse themselves, and be real radicals, they go around the block, to the Dillpickle. Mr. Johns, who is one of the co-operatives of the bookshop, is also one of the proprietors of the Dillpickle, a sort of restaurant, public forum, dance hall, and at present "the slum of Chicago," because some of its hangers-on were arrested as supposed bomb manufacturers during the recent I.W.W. trial.

It is a sort of debating club, *a la* Greenwich Village, with automobiles in front of it after ten p.m. when the rich come to see the poor, the law-abiding want to have a peek at the lawless, the properly married to see the free-lovers. . . . Chicago is very young, you know! It is in its bootees. All these "new ideas" are here in flower of springtime. I once said, "Were there no Greenwich Village, one would have to be invented." Chicago invented its own. The Dillpickle will have many competitors soon, under the signs of flowers, vegetables and animals. In a couple of years they will become stale canned goods. And then the empty cans will be consigned to the ash can. Greenwich Village all over again!

A column titled "Frederic Haskin's Letter" from the *Rock Island Argus* newspaper of Sept. 14th, 1920, detailing some Chicago bookstores, gives a bit of background of the new store. The article notes that it is run by a "gentle-voiced little lady, Mrs. Udell, assisted by her daughter Geraldine." It goes on, "Its history is an interesting example of idealism, which however much we may disapprove of it, we cannot help but admire. In times of great emergency they sold one of the valued books from their private library, 'feeling like cannibals when we did so,' says Mrs. Udell."

The Walden Book Shop was opened by the co-op group as a second shop[26] at 311 Plymouth Court. Both stores were to be run on a co-operative basis. When a shareholder bought a book at the shop, they would write your name and address on a form, and at the end of the year, a percentage of the profit of the purchase would be returned to them. The *Rock Island Argus* column notes, "So far the percentage returned to purchasers has been so low as to be negligible, but... the shops are already paying dividends to the stockholders."

The Publishers Weekly of April 16th, 1921, printed a notice:

> CHICAGO.—The Radical Book Shop is moving to a new and larger store at 826 North Clark Street on May 1.[27]

A book on the history of the co-operative movement in Illinois[28] praised the company founded by Anderson and

---

26 In January of 1927, an advertisement announced a "Removal Sale... before moving to 309 Plymouth Court". In June, the address was still listed as 307 Plymouth Court in a trade publication, but by October of that year, the address was listed as 311 Plymouth Court in an advertisement.

27 The September 1922 issue of *The Publishers Weekly* still listed the address as 867, but in October, it changed to 826.

28 *The Consumers Co-operative Movement in Illinois* by Colston Estey Warne (Chicago: University of Chicago Press, 1926).

BOOKS AND PAMPHLETS WHICH TELL THE truth. Send for catalogs. Radical Book Shop, Co-Operative, 867 North Clark St., Chicago, Ill.

▲ Classified advertisement placed in *The Nonpartisan Leader*, February 7th, 1921.

Cooper. They detailed that 225 shares were sold at $5 a piece but that there was a loss of $3,500 by 1922. A proposition to move the store to the "loop district" was opposed, and so stockholders of the co-operative, decided that because the Radical Book Shop ran at such a deficit, and only existed on profits of the Walden Book Shop, official ties should be severed. *The Publishers Weekly* for April 15th of 1922 carried the following notice:

> **Chicago, Ill.**—The Chicago Co-Operatives Book Store Company has sold out its interest in the Radical Book Shop located at 826 North Clark Street.

Mrs. Udell[29] took back management of the shop once more, and Theron P. Cooper managed the Walden Book Shop.[30] It is unclear how long the Walden Book Shop was run as a co-operative.

The *Daily Worker* printed a celebratory notice on July 17th, 1924, noting that spinning off the Radical Book Shop helped its trajectory into commercial sucess two years later:

29 A February 26th, 1922, article in the *Chicago Evening American* gave Lillian's home address at the time as 168 W. Chicago Ave.

30 Co-operative opened a second store under the Walden name in 1924. A third was advertised as being opened in the Palmolive Building in 1929, and a fourth in the Michigan Square building at 546 North Michigan Avenue. The three-story storefront of the latter is famous for its art-deco facade.

Walden Cooperative Bookshop Wins

The Chicago Cooperative Book Stores Company, has just completed a thorly (sic) successful year. This happens to be the first financially successful year of its short four year's existence. Organised in April, 1920, the Chicago Cooperative Book Stores Company opened two bookshops, the "Radical Book Shop" and the "Walden Book Shop." In 1922, the first of these was sold to another concern and all attention given to the making the Walden Book Shop a genuine co-operative success.

▲ Walden Book Shop, Michigan Square Building, Chicago, 1931. This drawing of the art-deco facade by architects Holabird & Root is extremely close to what was built.

STUDIO PLAYERS

It was in July of 1922 that an announcement was made about the formation of the Studio Players in *The New Majority*[31] journal:

> Once in a while comes a period in which the commercial theaters let a few plays through that attack existing institutions or reflect on the present social or industrial order. For instance, at present the big theaters are running *Liliom, Anna Christie, The Hairy Ape*. This must not lead us to believe that the theater is a free forum for expression.
>
> It is the little theater movement that blazes the trail in the effort to overcome the commercial censorship which (for varying reasons) keeps many plays off the stage. In Chicago a company has been formed called the Studio Players. Its home is in a little theater at the rear of the Radical Book Shop, 826 N. Clark street. Here, with all the intimate touch that is possible between players and audience in a room holding only fifty seats.
>
> Last week four performances were given of Ibsen's play, *The Lady From the Sea*. Not by any means the best of Ibsen's plays, still it is a powerful protest against matrimonial enslavement and the use of the nuptial contract to deprive parties thereto of exercise of free will for life.
>
> The presentation was earnest, the play was so difficult as to try the abilities of the cast to the utmost. The best work was done by Phyllis Udell,

31 *The New Majority* was available for sale at the Radical Book Shop.

Studio Players

IN

"DIFF'RENT"

A New England Tragedy in two acts

Eugene O'Neill

"Sweeps of Ninety-eight"

An Historical Comedy

John Masefield

Thursday Eve., November 2nd
Friday Eve., November 3rd
Saturday Eve., November 4th
Sunday Eve., November 5th

Curtain 8:15

AT

RADICAL PLAYHOUSE

826 North Clark Street

Tickets 50c —→ For sale at Radical Book Shop, 826 N. Clark St. and Walden Book Shop, 307 Plymouth Ct. and Box Office.

Press of S. Th. Almberg, 915-17 N. Wells St. 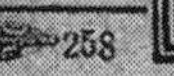 258

▲ Poster for a Studio Players performance of *Diff'rent* by Eugene O'Neill. Image courtesy of the Newberry Library.

who also had the most difficult role.

A positive review in *The New Majority* of September 2nd, 1922, detailed, in somewhat of a compliment, that the Studio Players gave a performance that was a "distinct advance over their work at the beginning of the summer season." The play this time was *The Importance of Being Earnest* by Oscar Wilde. "It was a snappy show, full of pep and fun," read the review, in a manner that sounds as if one was forced to satirize a review from the 1920s.

John Drury's 1928 book *Chicago in Seven Days*[32] has two characters pay a visit to the shop on Saturday:

> Reaching Chicago Avenue, we turned west and walked four blocks to the intersection of Clark Street and Chicago Avenue. Here, I conducted Anne half a block north and brought her to the Radical Book Shop, in the old North Side Turner Hall at 826 North Clark Street.
>
> "This is the home of the Studio Players," I said, "the oldest and most famous 'little theater' in the district, putting on its plays in a tiny theater at the rear of the book shop. As they have a bill of one-acters tonight, suppose we drop in and see what takes place."
>
> After the play was over, Anne remarked on the awkwardness of some of the youthful actors, but was impressed by the sincerity of all of them. I told her this "little theater" has been in existence at this place for almost ten years during which time it produced numerous recent New York plays which

32 *Chicago in Seven Days* (New York: R. M. McBride & Co., 1928).

S T U D I O   P L A Y E R S

in

"THE IMPORTANCE OF BEING EARNEST"

Oscar Wilde

(Cast in order of appearance:)

Lane (manservant)	Arthur Kramer
Algernon Moncrieff	Pierre Hunt
John Worthing J.P.	D. Cameron White
Lady Bracknell	Emily Richardson
Hon. Gwendolen Fairfax	Eulalie Burke
Miss Prism	Geraldine Udell
Cecily Cardew	Phyllis Udell
Rev. Canon Chasuble D.D.	Ernest Brady
Merriman (Butler)	Merle St. Leon

Act. 1. Algernon Moncrieff's Flat on Half Moon Street, W.

Act 11. Garden at the Manor House, Woolton.

Act 111. Garden room of the Manor House, Woolton.

Time: The present.

Place: London.

For information regarding the Studio Players, address Lilian Hiller Udell, 826 North Clark Street, or Phone Superior 9168.

failed to reach Chicago, such as Eugene O'Neill's *All God's Chillun Got Wings* and Elmer Rice's *The Adding Machine*. I added that that their repertory included plays by George Bernard Shaw, August Strindberg, Ibsen, Hauptmann, Chekhov, as well as the efforts of local playwrights like Logan Trumbull and Marion Strobel.

On March 28th, 1923, the Poetry Club of the University of Chicago was reported to have held a meeting at the Radical Book Shop, where Jessica North,[33] who was its president at the time, gave a reading.

33 North later succeeded Harriet Monroe as editor of *Poetry* magazine in 1936, after the latter's death, and co-edited the magazine with Peter De Vries from 1937 to 1942.

◂ Playbill for a Studio Players performance of *The Importance of Being Ernest* by Oscar Wilde. Image courtesy of the Newberry Library.

ROBOTS INVENTED FOR WEIRD COMMUNIST PLAY

One of my more absurd discoveries about the history of the Radical Book Shop is that in 1923, the Labor Defense Council staged a little theater performance of the science-fiction play *R.U.R.* Written by the Czech writer Karel Čapek, "*R.U.R.*" stands for Rossumovi Univerzální Roboti (Rossum's Universal Robots), a play that had premiered in a major theater in Chicago the year previously. It was performed by the Studio Players, including, of course, Geraldine, and directed by the Players' Guy Woodson. It was Čapek's play that introduced the word "robot" into the English language, deriving from a Czech word, *robota,* meaning "forced labor".

The *Daily Worker*'s hyperbolic announcement:

> The principal parts are being taken by actors and actresses of wide experience, who can be depended upon to put into the production all the force and fire and sarcasm and majesty that its Communist authors intended...
>
> The Labor Defense Council considers *R.U.R.* not only as a great drama but as an extraordinary piece of propaganda, one which cannot fail to burn its lesson deep into the mind of every proletarian. Thousands of workers are expected to witness the performances. The whole enterprise will be on a larger scale than anything of its kind ever attempted. All available resources will be mobilized to make it something which will be long remembered in the Chicago labor movement.

And then,

> **Six Robots Wanted.**
>
> To complete the cast, the Labor Defense Council is on the lookout for six sturdy Robots, to personify the product turned out in "Rossum's Universal Robot" factory. There is little or no speaking required of these "robots." A good robot—like a good wage slave—is one who does what he is told and says little. But in spite of the humbleness of their roles, the robots are as necessary to the cast of *R.U.R.* as the workers are to industry. The parts must be filled at once.

The notice ends,

> In the midst of the preparations for the staging of *R.U.R.*, the Studio Players, who will be the back bone of the production, are continuing their own performances of out-of-the-ordinary plays in their little theatre back of the Radical Book Shop. Their next production will be Bernard Shaw's "Man and Superman."

All radical politics tend to create small circles (often circular firing squads). Of note here is Lenetta M. Cooper, the wife of Theron Cooper, who worked at the Plymouth St. branch of the Walden Book Shop. Netta was one of the 21 persons on the national committee of the Labor Defense Council that staged the play. The L.D.C. was established as a fundraising group by the Communist Party of America in September 1922.

KENNETH REXROTH KISSES SISTER GERALDINE

In *An Autobiographical Novel* by Kenneth Rexroth, the poet details his meeting of Sherwood Anderson in 1924. At the time, he was borrowing books from the library on German Expressionism, Italian Futurism, and the Symbolists. His dive into radical art was fueled by discovering the bookstore:

> About this time I discovered a source for the kind of books I wanted to read. The Radical Book Shop in the old North Side Turner Hall on North Clark Street started importing the avant-garde poetry of the Twenties from France and Germany and Russia. In a short while they were also getting American and English books, published by the first Paris-Americans. I bought them all, and I only wish I had saved them, because they'd be worth a lot of money today. Nobody else wanted them, and I usually got them at considerable discount.
>
> The Radical Book Shop had a Little Theater with a tiny stage in the back room. Here I acted in Shaw and Wedekind. For some reason I was usually cast as an old man, and while still in high school, heavily and amateurishly made up with Oxford glasses on a ribbon, I made a most flatulent Roebuck Ramsden. The Radical Book Shop was run by a frail, white-haired widow, Mrs. Udell, who was totally blind, and who was always accompanied by a blonde and a brunette daughter at her right and left hand, Geraldine and Phyllis. They had grown up in the Little Theater in the back room and knew by heart all the lines

> of all the desperate young misses in all the Theater of Revolt. I think they fancied themselves as considerably higher-brow Gish sisters, with a dash of Nazimova, and they were, rather. The mother was a Sibylline and sepulchral character straight out of a Greek oracle. She said almost nothing, and what she did say was ambiguous and intimidating. Phyllis was too nervous, too much on the Ida Rubinstein ride for me, but Geraldine was even calmer and more collected than her mother and not at all cryptic. All it ever came to was a kiss or two on the stage in a Wedekind tragedy of youngsters like ourselves.

It was possibly at the Radical Book Shop where he picked up a copy of Wyndham Lewis' journal *The Blast*.

„New York Call" und „Milwaukee Leader".

Allen Genossen und Lesern zur Kenntnis, daß der „New York Call" und der „Milwaukee Leader", die größten sozialistischen Tageszeitungen in diesem Lande, in englischer Sprache, an folgenden Plätzen jeden Tag zu haben sind:

Clarion Book Shop, 204 N. Clark Straße.

Proletarian Book Shop, 1237 W. Madison Straße.

Radical Book Shop, 867 N. Clark Straße.

Machinists' Hall, 113 S. Ashland Blvd.

▲ Announcement from *Vorbote* (Chicago, Illinois), May 2, 1920, pg. 6.

VINCENTE MINNELLI STARTS AND QUITS ACTING 

The third husband of actress Judy Garland, Vincente Minnelli, recalls his brief stint in the theater of the Radical Book Shop whilst growing up in Chicago in his memoir, *I Remember It Well:*[34]

> I even made a half-hearted attempt at acting. A blind woman came in one day, accompanied by a young girl, asking to borrow some props from Mr. Frazier.[35] She was with a group which put on plays in a theater behind the Radical Book Shop on North Clark Street. They were doing an O'Neill one-acter. "Would you like to join our group?" the

34 Minnelli, Vincente, *I Remember It Well* (Garden City: Doubleday & Company, Inc., 1974).

35 Mr. Frazier was the head of the display department of Marshall Field, a Chicago department store. Mr. Minnelli got a job at as Mr. Frazier's fourth assistant in his late teens.

"THE GROWING DAWN"

A PLAY IN THREE ACTS

Dedicated to LILLIAN HILLER UDELL

Whose Eyes of Mind See The Growing Dawn.

▲ Title and dedication for the play *The Growing Dawn* by Edward Chichester Wentworth. Published in *The Valley of Enna & Other Poems of 1922.The Growing Dawn, and Spirit of the Lower North Side; Plays of 1922* (Chicago: Covici-McGee, 1923). Mr. Wentworth was a member of the Chicago Ethical Society, and the play featured Radical Book Shop regulars as characters, including Malfew Seklew.

woman asked.

I reported to the theater to read for one of the lesser parts, and went into rehearsal the same night. It was one of O'Neill's greatest exercises in foreboding doom... a retired sea captain going mad, along with his son... given to many pregnant pauses, it seemed to me, and to frequent trips to the roof in order to symbolically find the meaning of life, a vision he would receive through his trusty telescope. I was going mad along with the captain and his son.

Next door was a dance hall separated from the theater by a plywood partition. We were blitzed by the yelling and cussing that accompanied the frequent free-for-alls on the other side of that thin wall. Sometimes, when some battler was knocked against the partition, it looked as if we would be brought into the action... I fully expected it to happen whenever that wall finally toppled.

One evening, an Irishman came into the theater. He'd just been released from jail after serving a sentence for some sort of organized anarchy. "We won't stop," he screamed, "until we hang every capitalist from the highest lamp post!" The troupe reacted to his ranting as if it were a commonplace occurrence, which it probably was, meeting his outburst with desultory cheers. That did it for me. I packed my gear and walked out, turning my back on acting forevermore. If the performing arts lost a bright light you can blame it on the Bolsheviks.

THE STUDIO PLAYERS

perform at

THE RADICAL PLAY-HOUSE

826 North Clark St.

Saturday and Sunday Nights

Recent productions have included plays by

EUGENE O'NEIL
H. L. MENCKEN
FLOYD DELL
AUGUST STRINDBERG
BERNARD SHAW
ALFRED KREYMBORG
JOHN SYNGE
HENRIK IBSEN
BJÖRNSTIERNE BJÖRNSON

Arrangements may be made for special performances at private residences

TELEPHONE SUPERIOR 9168

THE RADICAL BOOK SHOP

826 NORTH CLARK ST. CHICAGO

▲ Advetisement from *Poetry*, Vol.3 No.6, March 1924

A JOB FOR GERALDINE, A FEW MORE PLAYS, THEN...NOTHING

Harriet Monroe, founder and then-editor of *Poetry* magazine, hired Geraldine as her personal assistant in 1925, but "Gerry" continued acting in plays put on by the Studio Players, often directed by her sister.

The *Daily Worker* printed this notice in 1925:

> Meeting of North Side workers will be held tonight at the Radical Book Shop. 826 N. Clark St., at 8 p.m. under the auspices of the North Side Branch of the International Labor Defense.
>
> All readers of the DAILY WORKER residing in the North Side are welcomed at this gathering which will be of great interest, dealing as it will with the subject of the defense of class-war prisoners in America.
>
> Admission will be free. The speaker of the evening will be S. T. Hammersmark[36] who will explain why the workers must organize for their defense on the political field.

The Daily Worker of Thursday, October 12th, 1926, had a notice that the Studio Players were performing *The Adding Machine* by Elmer Rice as a fundraiser for them at the Douglas Park Auditorium but that they "give performances

36 Samuel "Sam" Tellefson Hammersmark was a lifelong radical, having been deeply affected as a teenager by the Haymarket events, and was one of the founders of the I.W.W. and a figure in the American Communist Party. He was listed as the "manager" on the letterhead of the Workers' Book Store at 19 S. Lincoln Street in Chicago on a letter dated December 16th, 1926. In his later years, Hammersmark worked as the manager of the Modern Bookstore, the Communist Party's book shop in Chicago.

every Saturday and Sunday night at the Radical Book Shop, 826 North Clark Street."

A February 6th, 1927, article in the *Chicago Tribune* noted that the Dil Pickle and Radical Book Shop were two of the oldest of the Bohemian scene in "Tower Town," a district around the Chicago Water Tower.

Later that year, in the same paper, it was announced that the play *The Cad*, written by Marion Strobel (known by "society" as Mrs. James Herbert Mitchell, her husband being a famous dermatologist), was well received by an audience of social radicals and social elites. It was performed by the Studio Players. Harriet Monroe was in attendance, and Geraldine Udell played the female lead in the production[37].

Though I don't have infomation on when they left and what they did while away, on September 19th, 1930, Lillian, Phyllis, and Geraldine arrived at the port of New York on the ship "Volendam" from Boulogne-sur-Mer, France. Lilian was 58 and the girls both in their late 20s and unmarried. They lived at 205 Ontario St. in Chicago at the time.

In November 14th, 1930, a newspaper account of the death of Theron P. Cooper was published. A six-page letter was found in which the author detailed his slow death as he was overtaken by gas left on in the kitchen. "I have heard that gas was an easy and quick way to die, but I have been writing now for 45 minutes and am still able to scribble." His brother Kenneth L. Cooper denied the accusation of suicide, saying he found his brother in the garage, overtaken by automobile exhaust fumes.

An announcement of September 24th, 1932, detailed a

---

37 Marion Strobel was an "associate editor" of *Poetry* magazine for a short while. Geraldine Udell would step in as editor when Harriet was travelling in the 1930s, and was officially the "Business Manager" of *Poetry* in April of 1947.

bankruptcy auction of Walden Book Shops[38] to be held at 546 N. Michigan Ave.[39]

In 1933, the Dil Pickle Club was shut down using an ordinance prohibiting dancehalls from being within 100 feet of a church.[40]

38 There is no connection to the national chain named "Waldenbooks".

39 Theron's widow, Lenetta "Netta" M. Cooper, who was involved in the Labor Defense Council, had worked at Walden at Plymouth St. location and opened a new bookstore in 1932 at the University Club on S. Michigan Ave. named the Concord Book Shop. It later merged with Main Street book store on N. Michigan Ave in 1953. For many years, she worked as a talent scout for Harper & Bros., which is now HarperCollins.

40 *The Rise & Fall of the Dil Pickle Club* (Chicago: Charles H. Kerr, 2013).

REBELLION
AND
SONGS OF LOVE AND REBELLION
ON SALE AT:

Staub's Newsstand, Common, near Carondelet, City.
Holle's Newsstand, 613 Camp, City.
Radical Book Shop, 817 1-2 N. Clark Street, Chicigo, Ill.
M. Aldeman's Book ,Shop, 291 Tremont street, Boston, Mass.
Book Omnorium, 1350 Fillmore street, San Francisco, Cal.

▲ An advertisement from Wobbly poet Covington Hall's journal *Rebellion: Made up of Dreams and Dynamite* Vol. 1 No. 3 (New Orleans: May, 1915). Hall, who wrote under many pen names, was a great promotor of Ragnar Redbeard's work, and made the phrase "MIGHT IS RIGHT" a cornerstone of his early propaganda work. Hall's most widely reprinted poem, a standard song in the I.W.W. songbook for half a century, was titled "Might Is Right" and was a simple reworking of Redbeard's poem "The Logic of To-Day." That poem was featured in Hall's book *Songs of Love and Rebellion* (New Orleans: John J. Weihing Printing Co., 1915).

▲ Photo from a *Poetry* magazine party, circa 1952. First row: Marion Strobel, Geraldine Udell. Second row: George Dillon, Fanny Butcher, Peter De Vries. Image care of The Poetry Foundation.

The Radical Book Shop made no more news, at least none available to me. Lillian died in 1935, at her house at 523 Belden Ave. The obituaries that ran in the *Chicago Tribune* and *New York Times* were similar. The former called her the "'godmother' of most of Chicago's 'hobohemia,'" whereas the *New York Times* referred to her as the "mother of Chicago's bohemia." One is not the same as the other, and the local paper is a better picture of the reality. Both of them attribute her with being a founder of the Dil Pickle Club, which she was certainly present at and partook in.

A July 19th, 1940, article titled "A Feather from the Molted Left Wing"[41] in the *Chicago Tribune* tells a plausible story about the gradual disappearance of the shop:

> Phyllis and Geraldine Udell were hawking pacifist literature on the streets during World War I, when other girls of their age were playing hopscotch. Between them and their mother they hatched a plan

41 Strangely, it was signed "Archie the Cockroach II", a reference to the satirist Don Marquis' famous characters Archy and Mehitabel. The same name was attributed to a letter writer that reminisced about the Yellow Kid at the Dil Pickle Club in the same paper a week before.

▲ Ticket to a performance of a recital at the Dil Pickle Club. Of note is the logo used on the 1927 Dil Pickle Press edition of *Might is Right* by Ragnar Redbeard.

> for putting on dramas of social significance. A stage was set up in the rear of the bookshop and, as the audiences grew, the shop was pushed out of the way until it occupied little more than a window space.

Phyllis eventually married a man named George Hanson and was still directing plays into the 1940s with the Douglas Smith Players, an acting group for youths funded by the Douglas Smith Foundation.

Geraldine had been the personal assistant to Harriet Monroe for a decade until the latter's death in 1935 and became the Business Manager of *Poetry*. In that role, she was in regular correspondence with some of the great poets of the day, and you will find her name in collections of letters and memoirs ranging from Una Jeffers and Theodore Rothke to Margaret Walker and Edgar Lee Masters.

In 1948, the poet Kenneth Rexroth published a poem titled "A Christmas Note for Geraldine Udell." The poem itself mentions recalling Geraldine in a play he refers to as *Gas* and her performance as the "heroine on the eve of explosion." It was one of a handful of his poems that touched upon the I.W.W. The first four lines contain a tribute to radicals who spent time at the Radical Book Shop: "Debs, Berkman, Larkin, Haywood, they are dead now."

When Karl Shapiro became editor of *Poetry* in 1950, his first decision was to fire "Gerry" Udell.[42]

42 *Dear Editor: A History of Poetry in Letters* edited by Joseph Pariri and Stephen Young (New York: W.W. Norton & Company, 2002).

AFTERWORD: A PLACE FOR THEIR STORY

As a bibliophile with a passion for fringe literature, discovering the history of this Chicago bookstore, barely mentioned in modern work, was personally fulfilling. The stories that unfolded there, and the ripples that undulated from its impact, overlap and intermingle with others studied by the Union of Egoists project that I began in 2016 with Trevor Blake.

Lillian Udell herself deserves a dedicated study. The blind, erudite woman standing for herself, her family, and her passions is too romantic a story to merely be contained in the history of her bookstore and theater. The family and their bookstore had a demonstrable impact on the wider culture, politically, artistically, and intellectually. It will take someone able to travel and dig into regional archives and libraries to do it full justice.

While there may be more to learn about the Udells and their store, I hope this first history serves as a beginning for that, not to mention an informative aside for those studying the lives and deeds of the many figures that walked in and out of the doors of that Radical Book Shop.

If you have images, text, or any other information about the Udells or their bookstore that isn't included in this book, please reach out to me directly:

editor@UnionOfEgoists.com

THE STYLUS.

A Journal of Impressions.

VOLUME I. NO. I. MEADVILLE, PA., APRIL, 1896. 10 CTS. A COPY. $1.00 A YEAR.

THE STYLUS is published on the first of every month. Address all communications to THE STYLUS, Meadville, Pa.

Edited by LILIAN HILLER UDELL.

CONTENTS.

IT IS perhaps characteristic of the French and English temperaments, that while among the former people the theatre is almost always a source of artistic as well as sensuous delight, among the latter every manifestation of native dramatic genius has been irregular and spasmodic, periods of intense creative energy alternating with periods of hopeless inanity.

In his interesting review of the modern English drama, in the January issue of *Cosmopolis*, Mr. Arthur B. Walkley tells us that since the days of Sheridan, the English stage has languished in one of its sterile intervals. In place of classic tragedy and brilliant comedy, there have been only melodramatic representations of the commonplace, or trivial and tasteless imitations of their Gallic neighbors. The play house has been regarded as a place of amusement, and very inspid has been the amusement it has provided. Men and women of taste disappeared from among its patrons, to make room for the less thoughtful and more easily pleased.

Of late, however, all this has been changed, It seems to have occurred to the men and women of taste that they too wished to be amused. As there was no native drama, they accepted a foreign product, the plays of Henrik Ibsen.

The English are nothing if not earnest. No wonder, then, that they responded to the tragic earnestness, the deep questionings of the Scandinavian dramatist. Of course, they did not yield without a struggle. We all remember the curious specimens of journalistic billingsgate preserved for us by Mr. Bernard Shaw. As Mr. Walkley observes: "The almanac makers predicted that the end of all things was at hand."

But the end of all things has not yet come, only the end of the long ascendency of Sardou and Scribe in the British theatre.

Mr. Arthur Wing Pinero and Mr. Henry Arthur Jones hasten to avail themselves of this new condition of affairs. It was in "The Profligate" (1889) that Mr. Pinero first showed Ibsenian tendencies; but it was not until the presentation of "The Second Mrs. Tanqueray" (1893) that he established his claim to be considered a genuine disciple of his northern master. This drama depicts the disastrous consequences of an experiment in marriage. In his succeeding play, "The Notorious Mrs. Ebbsmith," we see the still more tragic consequences of an experiment in free love.

Despite the debt he owes to Ibsen, Mr. Pinero has succeeded in creating a live English drama.

When will some gifted American follow the example of Mr. Pinero and give us a native drama that shall truly interpret us to ourselves, and to other nations?

On his former visit to the United States Paderewski surpassed all other living pianists. This time he surpasses himself. Would that all America might have the delight of hearing this successor of Rubenstein,

▲ Front page of *The Stylus*, Vol. 1 No. 1, April 1896. Care of Yale University Library.

APPENDIX

IBSEN'S LATEST UTTERANCE
Liberty Vol. 11, No. 4 (Whole No. 316), (June 29, 1895)

(EDITORIAL)
The Stylus Vol. 1, No. 1 (April 1896)

CRITICISM AS AN ART
The Stylus Vol. 1, No. 1 (April 1896)

IS THOMAS HARDY A PESSIMIST?
The Stylus Vol. 1, No. 1 (April 1896)

OUR NATIONAL LITERATURE
The Stylus Vol. 1, No. 1 (April 1896)

STEPHEN CRANE AS NOVELIST AND POET
The Stylus Vol. 1, No. 1 (April 1896)

(NOTE ON NIETZSCHE)
The Stylus Vol. 1, No. 1 (April 1896)

THE LOVE AFFAIRS OF A BIBLIOMANIAC
The Stylus Vol. 1, No. 1 (April 1896)

FURTHER IMPRESSIONS
The Stylus Vol. 1, No. 1 (April 1896)

JOTTINGS
The Stylus Vol. 1, No. 1 (April 1896)

"OUR LITERARY IDOLS"

Freeport Daily Democrat (February 12, 1897)

IN BEHALF OF THE EDUCATED BLIND

Waturbury Republican (July 16, 1910)

REVOLUTIONARY ESSAYS

The International Socialist Review, Vol. XV, No. 1 (July 1914)

AN AMERICAN ANARCHIST

The Little Review, Vol.1, No. 7 (October 1914)

BOOK REVIEWS FROM THE INTERNATIONAL SOCIALIST REVIEW

International Socialist Review (September 1905–October 1914)

NOTICES FROM THE DAY BOOK

The Day Book (March 1915–December 1916)

IBSEN'S LATEST UTTERANCE 

Is Henrick Ibsen a teacher? If so, what does he teach? These were the questions that presented themselves to me, despite all previously formed judgements, as I closed the little volume containing the latest of his social plays, *Little Eyolf*.

In *Brand*, we see the Christian ideal of self-sacrifice pursued unflinchingly to its legitimate culmination in sublime yet tragic failure. "What a satire on Altruism!" exclaims the Egoist.

In *Peer Gynt*, the attempt to self-realization resolves itself into miserable inanity, an end possessing none of the sublimity, but all of the tragedy, which had characterized the former poem. "What a tremendous commentary on selfishness!" cry the delighted Altruists.

"But you must read *Ghosts*," chimes in a worshiper of nature, "if you would know what fate awaits those who prostrate themselves in submission to the moral law."

"Read *Rosmersholm*," gravely answers the moralist, "and learn the fearful penalties that attend any infringement of that law."

The invincible protest of humanity against Christianity, which rings like a peal of martial music through every scene of *Emperor and Galilean*, dies away in the despairing confession that "the Galilean has conquered."

Master-builder Solness scales the height to which his fair friend has incited him, but death comes to turn his victory into a ghastly jest.

It is not until we try to fathom the meaning of *Little Eyolf*, however, that our perplexity reaches its climax. In few of Ibsen's plays does the spell of his strange genius exert itself more powerfully; in none are the characteristic features of the author reproduced more signally, yet in none is the *denouement* so at valiance (if it is to be taken literally) with the entire spirit and letter of the master's earlier teachings.

The curtain rises upon a scene in which almost all the actors have become known to us. Alfred Allmers is Rosmer, transplanted into new conditions.

Rita, his wife, is the type of woman in whose delineation the dramatist most excels: beautiful; impetuous; passionate; with an intellect wherein the grossest misconceptions alternate with electric flashes of most penetrating insight; with a heart sometimes fierce, often tender, never tranquil.

In striking contrast with this rich, wild nature is that of Asta, the sister of Allmers.

Lovely and lovable always, she lives with but a single aim, that of bringing happiness to others.

She is one of those who, like the English poet's idea, "on tip-toe seem to touch upon a sphere too gross to tread." We venture to believe that if society were entirely made up of these angelic beings, the drama and the novel would never have come into existence.

In the centre of this little group stands Eyolf, the crippled child of Alfred and Rita, the object of his father's affectionate solicitude and his mother's jealous hatred.

Rita is passing through the old, well-nigh inevitable tragedy of a woman's life: that of seeing herself valued by her husband no longer as an individual to be respected but solely for the sale of her motherhood. She looks upon little Eyolf as having supplanted her in the heart where she would reign the undisputed queen.

After the boy's tragic death, however, the wife learns, to her horror, that her husband had at no time deeply and sincerely loved her. He married her, in part, because she was entrancingly beautiful but still more because of her gold and her green forests.

On the same day, Allmers discovers that Asta is only his foster sister and perceives that the love which he has pledged to the one woman he has given to the other. Asta, seeing his passion for her, and knowing it to be reciprocal, thinks instantly of the unhappy Rita. To save her friend, she gives her hand in marriage to one whose love she does not pretend to return and leaves the man she loves alone with the being whose passionate devotion has become only a source of weariness and vexation. Alfred and Rita stand together, watching the steamer that bears her away from them, watching the death agony of life's dearest possibilities. The husband will fly for refuge of the solitudes of the mountains. The wife, bereaved of her love, will try to fill the void in her heart and life by devoting herself to the well-being of that fraction of bereaved humanity lyng nearest to her, the poor children of the village. When Alfred learns of this plan, he is struck with the sense of his nobleness and begs that he may remain at her side and aid in its execution. The dream-land of love and happiness is behind them. Its gates of pearl must remain closed and locked forever. But measureless fields of human need lie before them, inviting endless labor. They are on the eve of a long day's work, followed, perchance, by a contented evening whose sunset glow shall fall from the loving and approving eyes of Asta and little Eyolf.

And so, the curtain falls on three maimed lives; whole remnants are to be absorbed in the joyless service of mankind. Marriage, instead of a union sanctioned by the tie of mutual love, is a partnership for utilitarian purposes, philanthropic or otherwise.

Passion is an enemy to be feared, happiness an *ignis fatu-*

us never to be sought, and work our only refuge from despair.

Is this the final message from the author of *Ghosts* to the waiting world? Does he mean to tell us that all human endeavor ends inevitably in tragedy? Or is he, after all, simply an artist who reproduces phase after phase of life, with no deeper purpose than the faithful interpretation of nature? Should we read one of Ibsen's plays as we would look at a painting by Millet or listen to one of Wagner's operas: as an end in itself, a masterpiece of artistic power, rather than a vehicle of moral (or immoral) teaching?

I have long refused to entertain either of these conclusions. I am aware that, taken severally, the social dramas are capable of being interpreted as expressions of the most advanced social philosophy, but the veil of deep and constant gloom which enshrouds even his sublimist conceptions, the confutation of the doctrines embodied in any one of these dramas by the doctrines embodied in another, and, most of all, the deepening pessimism of *The Master Builder* and *Little Eyolf*, all these will lead the reader to question whether he has been right in regarding Ibsen as the high priest of Egoism.

It is perhaps characteristic of the French and English temperaments that while among the former people, the theater is almost always a source of artistic as well as sensuous delight, among the latter, every manifestation of native dramatic genius has been irregular and spasmodic, periods of intense creative energy alternating with periods of hopeless inanity.

In his interesting review of the modern English drama, in the January issue of *Cosmopolis*, Mr. Arthur B. Walkley tells us that since the days of Sheridan, the English stage has languished in one of its sterile intervals. In place of classic tragedy and brilliant comedy, there have been only melodramatic representations of the commonplace, or trivial and tasteless imitations of their Gallic neighbors. The playhouse has been regarded as a place of amusement, and very inspid has been the amusement it has provided. Men and women of taste disappeared from among its patrons, to make room for the less thoughtful and more easily pleased.

Of late, however, all this has been changed. It seems to have occurred to the men and women of taste that they, too, wished to be amused. As there was no native drama, they accepted a foreign product, the plays of Henrik Ibsen.

The English are nothing if not earnest. No wonder, then, that they responded to the tragic earnestness, the deep questionings, of the Scandinavian dramatist. Of course, they did not yield without a struggle. We all remember the curious specimens of journalistic billingsgate preserved for us by Mr. Bernard Shaw. As Mr. Walkley observes, "The almanac makers predicted that the end of all things was at hand."

But the end of all things has not yet come, only the end

of the long ascendency of Sardou and Scribe in the British theater.

Mr. Arthur Wing Pinero and Mr. Henry Arthur Jones hasten to avail themselves of this new condition of affairs. It was in *The Profligate* (1889) that Mr. Pinero first showed Ibsenian tendencies, but it was not until the presentation of *The Second Mrs. Tanqueray* (1893) that he established his claim to be considered a genuine disciple of his northern master. This drama depicts the disastrous consequences of an experiment in marriage. In his succeeding play, *The Notorious Mrs. Ebbsmith,* we see the still more tragic consequences of an experiment in free love.

Despite the debt he owes to Ibsen, Mr. Pinero has succeeded in creating a live English drama.

When will some gifted American follow the example of Mr. Pinero and give us a native drama that shall truly interpret us to ourselves and to other nations?

CRITICISM AS AN ART

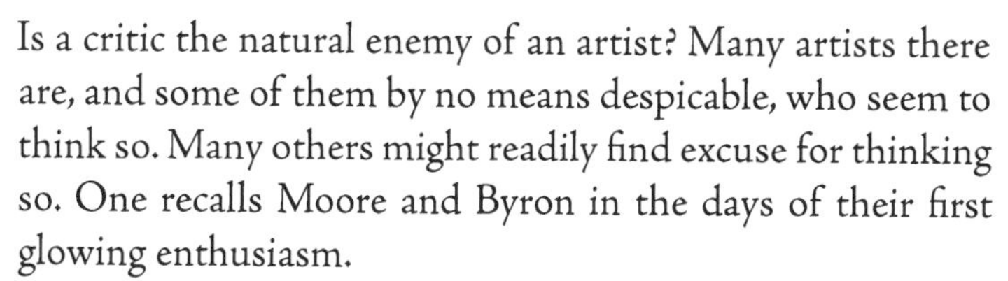

Is a critic the natural enemy of an artist? Many artists there are, and some of them by no means despicable, who seem to think so. Many others might readily find excuse for thinking so. One recalls Moore and Byron in the days of their first glowing enthusiasm.

How joyously they unsheathed their glittering steel for use against the unlucky reviewer.

George Eliot was constantly advised by Lewes not to read the criticism of her own writings.

Guy De Maupassant, to quote a more modern example, seems to have looked upon criticism as the spleen of little minds aspiring toward greatness yet incapable of it and hating the success they were powerless to emulate.

Turn to other forms of art. You will observe the same warfare waged with an even greater vehemence. Wagner among musicians, Ibsen among dramatists, Whistler and Monet among painters have found every step on their road to fame contested by an army of critics whose numbers and whose fury would have crushed less vigorous spirits utterly.

Now it is doubtless true that the protest raised by artists against their detractors frequently springs quite as much from motives of outraged vanity as from disinterested devotion to the cause of art. Neither can we deny that much of what passes for criticism deserves the worst that can be said of it by these or any other opponents. But are there not causes of antagonism between these two classes which lie deeper than all accidents of individual motive and method?

In estimating a novelist or poet, what is it that we require of him? First and before all things, we require that his work shall be done artistically. But of the critic, the man who is expected to understand and interpret a work of art, do we make a similar demand? By no means. Here our demands are as various as our temperaments.

Some of us insist that he shall be chiefly a moralist; others prefer the dainty epicure of the intellectual and æsthetic world, who interprets from the standpoint of "taste and sensibility," but always of an *a priori* taste and sensibility.

Then there are the few who view the critic as a scientist, but their number seems to be diminishing. Amid these widely differing standards of criticism, what is the one common quality or limitation which unites the critics in a common opposition to so much that is really great in art?

The first condition of artistic production is that its author be an objective thinker.

In other words, he must interpret the world in terms of universal consciousness. The moralist or æsthete interprets the world in terms of personal, local, or, at the most, national consciousness.

The artist is the creator of something original, novel; his critics are the worshipers of something ancient and familiar; still, we expect the critic sympathetically to understand and faithfully to interpret these products so alien to his mental habitudes. For this, something more is necessary than pre-existing standards and pre-conceived opinions.

The critic must live in his subject, know all its capabilities, make it part of himself.

Beneath a poem or statue or symphony, he must perceive its *raison d'etre*; beneath this, the man, the living personality who created it; beneath the man, the race, surroundings, and accidental circumstances of which he is the inevitable product. Such a critic will become one with the author. He will for the moment see with his eyes, think his thoughts, vibrate to his emotions. He will ask himself, What was it that the man of genius meant to express when he wrote the tragedy or painted the picture?

Once let him discover this secret, and every detail of picture or tragedy will break upon his consciousness, rich with previously undiscerned meaning and unnoticed suggestion. From an arrangement of words or of colors, he recreates a man, a city, a nation. In one word, if the critic would understand a man of genius: he must become like him, a creator, an artist.

France has been most happy in the possession of such critics.

The names of Saint-Beuve, Renan, Taine: will recur to everyone, as those of the men who have made of criticism not merely a science but a living and independent art.

Take a familiar example: Taine's *History of English Literature.*

Consider what the author has done. He has interpreted England to the world, and yet more, to herself. He has shown her what she is not, but he has also most brilliantly pointed out what she is. Thackeray is great not as a novelist but as the author of a most telling ethical satire. Byron reappears as a northern Skald transplanted into modern life. Even Shakespeare becomes a man again.

And all this is done from a standpoint wider than that of any special ethical or æsthetic cult, the standpoint of humanity, of universality, of truth.

Only give us such criticism as this, and we shall have an end of the unnatural divorce between the artist and the man who should be best qualified to comprehend his aims and their results.

Is Thomas Hardy a Pessimist? 

Ever since the appearance of *Tess of the D' Ubervilles,* public opinion regarding its author seems to have been considerably disturbed. Critics who had previously been vehement in his praise viewed this book as evincing a distinct loss not indeed of intellectual but of ethical and æsthetic grasp. Others, formerly indifferent, now maintained his indisputable title to a place among the foremost writers of English fiction. The appearance of *Jude the Obscure* deepened this disturbance into a very tempest of conflicting claims. It is the work of genius "entering on the last stages of senility," cries the ex-admirer. It is a masterpiece, exclaims a reviewer of a different mind. As to our own view, it is enough to observe that the might of a man may be safely measured by the number and strength of his enemies. Mr. Hardy's detractors prove, far more than do his eulogists, how genuine and permanent is the place he has won in his country's literature. We believe that *Jude the Obscure* has come to stay.

Our purpose, however, is not to enter upon the defense of one who needs no defenders. There is another question raised by Mr. Hardy's recent novels of which we would gladly hear some further discussion. Is Thomas Hardy a pessimist? Mr. Gosse apparently thinks that he is, so do a number of eminent and powerful critics for whose judgment we entertain the highest possible respect. Mr. Andrew Lang feels it so strongly that he refuses even to attempt the perusal of *Jude the Obscure.* Now, for aught we know to the contrary, Mr. Hardy's individual view of life may be that of Schopenhauer and Von Hartmann, but we do unhesitatingly affirm that neither from *Tess of the D' Urbervilles* nor from the succeeding novel do we draw any necessary conclusion in favor of pessimism.

Tragedy there undoubtedly is, and that of a most poignant quality. You turn over the last pages of *Jude the Obscure* with a feeling that life is only a mass of machinery, uncontrollable and irresponsible, ready at any moment to reduce any one of us to atoms. This you feel as you read the concluding chapters, but how is it afterwards, when you have found time for reflection? Does not another solution of the matter suggest itself to your mind? This "rectangular problem in failures," as the story has been called, is it an indictment against nature and destiny or against tradition and prejudice?

Recall the successive incidents in the life of the hero. Jude Fawley, an unsophisticated young workman of studious habits, is deliberately beguiled into an intimacy with a very sophisticated ex-barmaid. This is very unfortunate. But would it have been irretrievably so if the young man had not felt compelled to go through the form of marriage with a being separated from him by every instinct of her nature? Arabella was to Jude a woman whom he had wronged and to whom he owed all possible reparation. Jude was to Arabella a husband who should buy her new frocks. Just here, another thought occurs to us. Would this girl have sought such unnatural marriage if matrimony did not stand for the economic dependence of the woman? Suppose Arabella the wife were responsible for her own frocks as Arabella the maid had been. For these things, we blame not nature, nor fate, but an imperfect economic and social condition.

When the wife has grown weary of her unpractical husband and gone in search of new adventures, we find him restored to his study and his dreams of intellectual greatness. He goes to Christminster (Oxford) as a pilgrim to the holy place of his idolatry. Someday, he means to enter as a student.

When, however, he appeals for advice to the masters of its colleges, he is met with a polite version of the Church of England precept: "Do your duty in that station of life to which it has pleased God to call you." Might not this youth's future have been different if his appeal had been answered differently?

Later at Melchester, he goes with his cousin Sue Bridehead for a day's pleasure excursion; they miss the homeward-bound-train, and are compelled to pass the night with a hospitable cottager's family. Nothing could have been more unforeseen than this delay. Nothing could have been easier than for the principal of the school of which Sue was an inmate to have verified their explanation. Instead of this, the girl is made the object of cruel suspicion and humiliating punishment. Amid the deepening complications which follow, she is driven to fulfil a promise long ago repented and marry a man more than twice her years.

And now we come to the crowning mistake in a continuous tissue of mistakes. We refer to the period which followed the double divorce of Jude and Sue from their ill-chosen partners. Loving each other with a love that never for an instant wavered, they yet refused to legalize a marriage long since consummated in the hearts and lives of both. To this refusal, born of miserable and causeless doubt, might be traced the long train of misunderstandings, persecutions, and disasters that brought the woman to defilement and the man to death. In every one of these instances, the protest is directed not against nature, nor destiny, but against the errors of the individual and the prejudices of society. Personally, we may regret the unrelieved gloom of this narrative, but after all, the question is not whether the author be a pessimist or an optimist, whether we accept his views of life or reject them. Our province is rather to ask, Does he, or does he not, at all times hold the "mirror up to nature"?

OUR NATIONAL LITERATURE: STUDIES OF AMERICAN WRITERS, NO. 1

Recall to your minds the picture of the Western world bathed in the effulgent afterglow of the Renaissance. Recreate in fancy the sudden outburst of joyous activity, the free, spontaneous, and resistless bubbling-forth of the unexhausted, unpolluted fountains of young life in the sixteenth and throughout the opening years of the seventeenth century. See that life realizing itself, sometimes in deeds of heroism, sometimes in acts of lawlessness, uttering itself, in the pauses of its action, in poems, pictures, peerless dramatic creations, triumphant peals of religious music, and in scientific experiment and philosophic speculation, then breaking out once more into wars of conscience and wars of conquest, in which differences of religious conviction became often the cause, and quite as often the pretext for national hostility. Do this and you will have recreated the type of manhood that laid the foundations of a literature, as of a civilization, in the vast and trackless wilderness of America.

Have we, then, a literature in this new world? Has America made any distinctive contribution to the intellectual and artistic activities of mankind? If so, what is the nature and scope of that contribution?

For the creation of a literature, three conditions must be regarded as indispensable. The first of these is a superabundant vital energy, seeking an outlet through a thousand diverse channels. There must be deeds in whose mere rehearsal the tongue grows eloquent. There must be passions with power to disfigure or transfigure the soul, the lightnings and thunders of life as well as its sunlit days and nights resplendent with their crown of stars. The deepest ocean, the most mysterious cave, the heavenward-reaching mountain must not be left unexplored.

Yet vain is all this varied thought and sentiment and experience without the idea of the beautiful, whose chemistry crystallizes the spoken word, the falling tear into a jewel, or swells the trembling sigh into a song.

Finally, there must be liberty of movement, room for the individual to drink deep draughts of exhilarating air into his lungs, to grow up to the stature of the highest manhood.

Where these conditions prevail, we look for the epic poem, the tragedy, and, at last, the novel. We are never disappointed. We shall find these creations, at all times, keeping pace with the degree to which these conditions are fulfilled.

Has America fulfilled these conditions at any period of her history? To answer this question is the purpose of the present series of papers.

The ships that spread their sails in the prosperous harbors of merry England and plunged into the toil and tumult, the adventures and disasters, of the long voyage to the unknown land came freighted with passionate desires, boundless hopes, and dauntless determination, but to create a literature was furthest from the thoughts of these stern conquerors of hostile circumstances. Fallen fortunes were to be retrieved. Religious liberty was to be secured. A race was to be reclaimed from the darkness of heathendom. An empire was to be won.

The spirit of the rising nation was too civilized to find utterance in the rude minstrelsy of primitive nations, too rugged to command the facile and seductive graces, the subtile and varied insights into nature and humanity, that characterize *belle-lettres*.

Yet in spite of this, we shall find in our next paper the imperfect beginnings of what will develop into a national literature.

STEPHEN CRANE AS NOVELIST AND POET

In the February issue of *The Philistine*[43] I found, among other things, some verses by Stephen Crane. It may as well be confessed that up to that time, this young author had been but a name to me. Verses of his had appeared in various periodicals. I had read them, but somehow, they had left no lasting impression. With these, the case was different. Their charm was so potent, their symbolism so subtle, their melody so haunting!

Surely, here was a realization of Lowell's definition of poetry: "The art of making beautiful conceptions immortal by exquisiteness of phrase." They exhibited most of the defects of the modern decadent poetry, but they possessed also its virtues.

I instantly procured and read whatever of Mr. Crane's writings were available at the moment. The first to fall into my hands was that curious little volume of verses entitled *The Black Riders and Other Lines.*

The immediate effect of these was a distinct feeling of disappointment. Later, however, came a recognition of the originality and force of the conceptions that lie back of the always vigorous, often crude, sometimes artistic execution.

Among the many remarkable facts in the development of this young genius, not least remarkable is the very trivial part played by the power of love in all his imaginings. At times, the note of passion sounds in his verse, but it is passion as it has been seen, not necessarily felt, by the poet. Here, for instance, is a bit of love's philosophy that might easily have come from the inner consciousness of an imaginative youth, without recourse to any deep or intimate experience of life:

---

43 Union of Egoists published a history of this journal: *Elbert Hubbard's The Philistine: A Periodical of Protest (1895–1915)* by Bruce A. White (Baltimore: Underworld Amusements, 2018).

AND YOU LOVE ME?

I LOVE YOU.

YOU ARE, THEN, COLD COWARD.

AYE; BUT, BELOVED,
WHEN I STRIVE TO COME TO YOU,
MAN'S OPINION, A THOUSAND THICKETS,
MY INTERWOVEN EXISTENCE,
MY LIFE,
CAUGHT IN THE STUBBLE OF THE WORLD
LIKE A TENDER VEIL,—
THIS STAYS ME.
NO STRANGE MOVE CAN I MAKE
WITHOUT NOISE OF TEARING.
I DARE NOT.

IF LOVE LOVES,
THERE IS NO WORLD
NOR WORD.
ALL IS LOST
SAVE THOUGHT OF LOVE
AND PLACE TO DREAM.
YOU LOVE ME?

I LOVE YOU.

YOU ARE, THEN, COLD COWARD.

AYE; BUT, BELOVED—

Far deeper than his understanding of love is his appreciation of the religious conflict of our time. Without fear, and without disguise, he summons the God of traditional theology before the court of his own conscience and condemns him:

A SPIRIT SPED
THROUGH SPACES OF NIGHT;
AND AS HE SPED, HE CALLED,
"GOD! GOD!"
HE WENT THROUGH VALLEYS
OF BLACK DEATH-SLIME,
EVER CALLING,
"GOD! GOD!"
THEIR ECHOES
FROM CREVICE AND CAVERN
MOCKED HIM:
"GOD! GOD! GOD!"
FLEETLY INTO THE PLAINS OF SPACE
HE WENT, EVER CALLING,
"GOD! GOD!"
EVENTUALLY, THEN, HE SCREAMED,
MAD IN DENIAL,
" AH, THERE IS NO GOD!"
A SWIFT HAND,
A SWORD FROM THE SKY
SMOTE HIM,
AND HE WAS DEAD.

At moments, he is cynical yet laughs at his own cynicism:

ONCE THERE WAS A MAN,—
OH, SO WISE!

IN ALL DRINK
HE DETECTED THE BITTER,
AND IN ALL TOUCH
HE FOUND THE STING.
AT LAST HE CRIED THUS:
"THERE IS NOTHING,—
"NO LIFE,
"NO JOY,
"NO PAIN,—
"THERE IS NOTHING SAVE OPINION,
AND OPINION BE DAMNED."

One thinks of him as another Whitman, only subtilized and without a trace of that Greek enjoyment of life which rings through the song of the older poet. In both, there is the same breadth and virility of thought, the same disregard of form, the same suggestion of a tempestuous spirit. But in *The Black Riders and Other Lines,* I caught no note of the poet whose verse had so delighted me in *The Philistine.* As a poet, then, not less than as a novelist, Mr. Crane's later work shows a steady and rapid advance in the development of his powers.

In the latter phase of art, his success is so well known that perhaps I owe an apology for mentioning it here. It has been so sudden and complete that one is almost tempted to regret it. At twenty-four, to be lifted in a day from comparative obscurity to a place beside his country's most gifted novelists, to be feted, caressed, flattered, and what is even more flattering, to be read and sincerely admired by every one: surely this is a severe test of the personal, as well as the artistic qualities of the strongest individual. Yet this is the ordeal which the author of *The Red Badge of Courage* has been called upon to face. That Mr. Crane will justify the promise he has given, there seems no reason to doubt. Should he fail in this, it would be due not to a lowering of his aims but to the fact that he does not know the secret of his own power.

He is a spendthrift of genius. His imagination projects a scene; he transports himself into the midst of it, with all the abandon of youth. Sensations, ideas, emotions, images come thronging to his aid. As you read the opening chapters of *The Red Badge of Courage*, objects of interest rise on every side. Incident follows incident, humorous, pathetic, passionate, with a rapidity that is electrical. But this momentum bears you on past the climax of dramatic interest before the narrative has reached its conclusion. Treating, as he does, of an episode of the Civil War, the author has perhaps committed no serious fault through such prodigality.

The main action of the story covers a period of but a few days, and it would be difficult to point out a more interesting bit of psychological analysis than is portrayed for us in these few swift strokes. One admires the sustained intellectual vigor that keeps the author true to his main object amid all the temptations of the battle scenes he is depicting. Mr. Crane does not paint an ideal hero. He does better than this. He creates a new type in fiction, the real soldier. He does it so graphically and powerfully that the experienced veteran verifies it at a glance. For one of his years and experience, who has never seen a battle, to have penned the best existing description of the sensations of the individual soldier in the thick of the conflict shows a very high quality of imagination. Some of Mr. Crane's minor portraits are less convincing. The transformation of the "loud soldier" from a blustering, swaggering fellow into the most manly as well as the bravest of his regiment seems almost too sudden to be taken seriously.

When we recognize an artist, we find a certain pleasure in trying to discover his affinities. But it is somewhat difficult to determine those of Stephen Crane. His verses, especially the latest of them, would seem to place him among the writers of the Decadent school. His novel, on the contrary, reveals him as a psychologist, whose observation, though limited, is singularly true. Mr. Hamlin Garland may have been his model, as some critics have affirmed, but his place should be among the intellectual sons of Paul Bourget. When we view his writings in the ensemble, we abandon the attempt to classify him.

Who shall say what one so gifted and so versatile may not achieve! All hail, then, to the rising star of this young author's fame! May it herald the dawn of a new inspiration to American genius.

(NOTE ON NIETZSCHE)

Among the books announced for publication by Macmillan & Co., none deserve a warmer welcome than the works of Friedrich Nietzsche. Those who know of this brilliant but unhappy writer only through Max Nordau's misrepresentations have a totally inadequate idea of the place he holds in the literature and philosophy of Germany. His *Zarathustra* deserves to be ranked as one of the classics of the German language. In the whole range of Wagnerian criticism, we doubt if there is anything more interesting or suggestive than his contributions to the subject.

"THE LOVE AFFAIRS OF A BIBLIOMANIAC" BY EUGENE FIELD.

(CHAS. SCRIBNER'S SONS.)

The average man, and still more the average woman, is prodigiously flattered upon being taken into another's confidence. One esteems that other somewhat more highly than heretofore. One esteems one's self very much more highly because of such trust. Perhaps it is a similar feeling which renders us so responsive whenever an author tries to establish confidential relations with us by means of a diary or other form of public confession. We attend with boundless patience to long and detailed narratives of a kind extremely trying in private conversation.

In this way, we have come to know the philosophic speculations of Amiel, the religious struggles of the youthful Renan, the melancholy of Stephen Allard. Now that we have heard the experiences of philosopher, scholar, dreamer, and a host of others, why should we not also listen to the adventures of a book collector? So, at least, thought the late Eugene Field, and thus thinking, he gave to the world *The Love Affairs of a Bibliomaniac.*

In this case, we are not even threatened with weariness. Nothing could be more delightful than the privilege of conversing with the old man who is the imaginary narrator of these amours. The volume contains a series of reminiscences and observations connected with book hunting. Every conceivable variety of topic, from book sellers to Napoleonana, from the pleasures of angling to the odors exhaled by old books, is treated in the half-graceful, half-humorous vein so characteristic of the poet. There are verses too, scattered here and there throughout the volume. We cannot regard these verses as among the best of their author's pieces; still, we find in them all the genial and spontaneous warmth of feeling which, more than anything else, has endeared him to the hearts of his readers. No one but our old friend would have penned these lines celebrating his delight in the *Decamcron*:

One day upon a top-most shelf
  I found a precious prize indeed,
Which father used to read himself,
  But did not want us boys to read;
A brown old book of certain age
  (As type and binding seemed to show),
While on the spotted title page
  Appeared the name "Boccaccio."

I'd never heard that name before,
  But in due season it became
To him who fondly brooded o'er
  Those pages a belovèd name!
Adown the centuries I walked
  Mid pastoral scenes and royal show;
With seigneurs and their dames I talked—
  The crony of Boccaccio!

Those courtly knights and sprightly maids,
  Who really seemed disposed to shine
In gallantries and escapades,
  Anon became great friends of mine.
Yet was there sentiment with fun,
  And oftentimes my tears would flow
At some quaint tale of valor done,
  As told by my Boccaccio.

In boyish dreams I saw again
  Bucolic belles and dames of court,
The princely youths and monkish men
  Arrayed for sacrifice or sport.
Again I heard the nightingale
  Sing as she sang those years ago
In his embowered Italian vale
  To my revered Boccaccio.

And still I love that brown old book
  I found upon the topmost shelf—
I love it so I let none look
  Upon the treasure but myself!
And yet I have a strapping boy
  Who (I have every cause to know)
Would to its full extent enjoy
  The friendship of Boccaccio!

But boys are, oh! so different now
  From what they were when I was one!
I fear my boy would not know how
  To take that old raconteur's fun!
In your companionship, O friend,
  I think it wise alone to go
Plucking the gracious fruits that bend
  Where'er you lead, Boccaccio.

So rest you there upon the shelf,
  Clad in your garb of faded brown;
Perhaps, some time, my boy himself
  Shall find you out and take you down.

> Then may he feel the joy once more
> That thrilled me, filled me years ago
> When reverently I brooded o'er
> The glories of Boccaccio.

In these reminiscences, woman finds herself in a somewhat unusual position. It is not that the old book-lover was a hater of women. On the contrary, he cherished a tender regard for several of them. There was Captivity Waite, the little friend of his childhood, who helped him to discover the *New England Primer.* Of her, he gives the following quaint description:

> A sixteenmo, if you please, fair to look upon, of clear, clean type, well ordered and well edited, amply margined, neatly bound, a human book whose text, as represented by her disposition and her mind, corresponded felicitously with the comeliness of her exterior.

Later comes the beautiful Yseult, or Fiammetta, as he loves to call her:

> "Had Fiammetta been a book, ah, unfortunate lady! had she but been a book she might still be mine, for use to care for lovingly and to hide from profane eyes and to attire in crushed levant and gold and to cherish as a best beloved companion in mine age! Had she been a book she could not have been guilty of the folly of wedding a yeoman of Lincolnshire—ah me, what rude awakenings too often dispel the pleasing dreams of youth."

Finally, we catch a glimpse of Fanchonette, "the dainty coquettish Gallic maiden" crowned with a garland of Béranger's poetry.

There are occasional jests at the expense of wives and maiden ladies.

Here, it must be confessed, the author is less happy than usual. These classes have so often been made the target of newspaper witticisms that to say anything original on this subject might well tax the invention of a greater genius than Mr. Field.

What lends to this book its pecular interest is the knowledge that its preparation was a labor of love, conceived years ago and executed during his last months, when ill health had unfitted him for more arduous labors. Its nineteenth chapter was written two days before his death. The verses at its conclusion, supposed to be those of his friend Judge Methuen, were the last ever penned by the poet's hands. But one more chapter remained to be written, of which the old bibliomaniac's death was to have been the theme. Of his own death, which was utterly unexpected, his loved books were the only witnesses, and they will never tell their secret. We lay down the volume with a smile and a tear for the poet of books, of woman, and of that host of little ones whose tribute of love would mean more to him than the proudest niche in the poets' corner of Westminster Abbey.

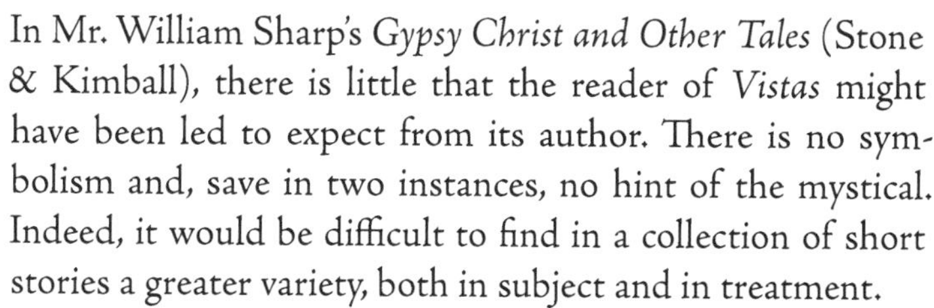

In Mr. William Sharp's *Gypsy Christ and Other Tales* (Stone & Kimball), there is little that the reader of *Vistas* might have been led to expect from its author. There is no symbolism and, save in two instances, no hint of the mystical. Indeed, it would be difficult to find in a collection of short stories a greater variety, both in subject and in treatment.

There are, in all, seven tales, covering almost as many phases of life and local color. We are transported from the Thames to the Adriatic, from an old English country house to the Arabian desert, and in each new scene, our guide moves as one to whom nothing is unfamiliar. In these tales, the author's manner varies with the scene he is painting.

It is almost inevitable from the very nature of such attempts that their results should prove very unequal in power and interest. Mr. Sharp has been no more and no less fortunate than others in this respect.

We like best "The Lady in Hosea." Its realism is delightful in quality, and its denouement is most original and unexpected. "Madge o' the Pool" has even greater possibilities, but toward the close, it loses much in dramatic power. "Froken Bergliot" is a genuine idyl. It is what, according to Milton, all true poetry must be, "simple, sensuous and passionate." The "Gypsy Christ," which gives the volume its title, relates the legend of Kundry, the Gypsy girl who laughed at the Christ on his way to crucifixion, and of the curse that ever afterward blasted the lives of her descendants.

* * * * *

Less unequal in merit, but also less powerful than Mr. Sharp's collection, is another little book of short stories, *Black Spirits and White*, by Ralph Adams Cram (Stone & Kimball). In a postscript the author says,

> There seem to be certain well-defined roots existing in all countries, from which spring the current legends of the supernatural; and therefore for the germs of the stories in this book the author claims no originality. These legends differ one from the other only in local color and in individual treatment. If the author has succeeded in clothing one or two of these norms in some slightly new vesture, he is more than content.

To the success of his attempt, most readers will gladly testify. We confess, however, that we might have experienced a more delicious thrill if we had heard less of sapphire seas, golden sunlight, violet mountains. It is too much like saying green trees, white snow, red blood, etc.

Landscape painting requires a high order of ability, and genius is no less rare here than in other forms of art. But if we cannot have genius, let us at least have novelty.

We shall forget as quickly as possible Mr. Cram's environment descriptions, but we shall take pleasure in remembering some of his ghosts, especially the beautiful but unfortunate Sister Maddelena, whose plaintive whisper echoes through the ages, "I cannot sleep."

* * * * *

Le Ventre De Paris (Neely), a novel of the Parisian markets, displays all of M. Zola's wonted powers of observation and description. We cannot help shrinking from the intolerable vividness of some of the pictures. The most sickening details of life in a pork shop are dwelt upon with wearisome persistence.

But the author paints these things not because he finds such scenes congenial: rather for the reverse reason. They weigh upon his senses. They torture his sensibilities. Everywhere, he shows himself capable of the most delicate sentiments, the noblest morality.

Whenever he alludes to the fat bourgeois, and his sleek, well-fed household, it is with an undertone of irony, while the half-starved dreamer and the not less impecunious artist are portrayed with the sympathy that rises from personal affinity alone.

No doubt, the book will be welcomed by many American readers, in spite of the unfortunate title, *The Fat and the Thin,* imposed upon it by the translator, E. A. Vizetelly.

* * * * *

Readers of Mrs. Burnett's earlier novels have been interested to observe her in her new role, as a writer of historical romance. *A Lady of Quality* (Scribner) has come as a pleasurable surprise to those who have grown weary of the sentimentalism of *Little Lord Fauntleroy*.

Her delineation of life in the early part of the eighteenth century is admirable. Her handsome, dashing heroine captivates, even while she offends our fastidious nineteenth century sense. From first to last, the interest of the story never flags.

Mr. Charles Dudley Warner, in *Harper's* for March, indulged in some rather caustic observations on the tendency of recent popular fiction. He is irritated by its "tragic" tone. He is irritated still more by its fatalism. Mr. Warner does not object to Greek tragedy. True, it recognized a fate but only such a fate as the Theologian might approve. The guilty were always punished, and the innocent vindicated, with a sort of clockwork regularity. The fate of the moderns is a mere mechanical law that never pauses in its operations to inquire into the guilt or innocence of its victims. If Mr. Warner will blot out the discoveries of science, and the experience of twenty-five hundred years, perhaps our novelists may regain the childlike faith he seems so much to admire.

Our feminine readers may be interested to know that the late Alexandre Dumas was not a woman-hater, as has commonly been asserted. He was an ardent believer in the possibilities of the sex. In a letter to a feminine friend (Mr. Sherard gravely informs us). the dramatist maintains that woman is physically as well as intellectually the superior of man. Are we supposed to take this seriously? We cannot help suspecting that M. Dumas was trying to flatter his fair correspondent. The equality of the sexes it is good to recognize, but woman's superiority is as false and absurd as man's superiority. Women are tired of compliments. They want something better.

Miss Harriet Munroe realizes six thousand dollars for her *Columbian Ode*, while Paul Verlaine, the greatest of recent French poets, never received more than five francs for a single poem. The moral is...but we refrain.

Herr Busoni, in his tour through the various European

cities, is meeting with somewhat unequal success. In Berlin, there are those who see in him, after Paderewski, the most gifted pianist alive. It is said that those who appreciated him most when he was a resident of the United States would be amazed at his marvelous development since that time. From Frankfurt, we hear that his playing in that city was coldly received and was destitute of any magnetic quality.

Speaking of publishers' announcements, a translation of Sonia Kovalevsky's novel *Vera Barantzova* is promised by Lamson Wolfe & Co. This news will be greeted with pleasure by those who enjoyed her autobiographical sketch, *The Raevsky Sisters*.

It is not often that genius is transmitted from parent to child. An exception to this rule is Mme. Judith Gautier, daughter of the distinguished novelist. The French Academy crowned her novel *Sœur du Soleil*, and the interpretations of Oriental life in her plays are said to be realistic in the extreme. She possesses great beauty and always appears attired in Japanese costumes.

Why have we raised Eleonora Duse to the first place in our admiration? It is not because she faithfully reflects the dramatist's conception of "Camille" or of "Magda." It is because while on the stage, she is "Camille," she is "Magda." Artistic simulation, however perfect, could never produce such painful exhaustion as Mme. Duse reveals at the close of each performance.

"Our Literary Idols"[44]

An Interesting Lecture by Mrs. Lillian Hiller Udell, the Blind Editor of *Stylus*.

The Speaker: An Iconoclast, but a Graceful and Refined One, and a Cultured Woman.

It would have been difficult for the Rev. George Brayton Penney to have found for last night's lecture, in the course prepared for the People's church, a more charming, graceful speaker than the slim little woman who hid her blindness behind a pair of black spectacles, Lillian Hiller Udell, who, in spite of an affliction that renders most people that suffer from it absolutely helpless, is an active worker in that field where it would naturally be thought sight is indispensable—journalism. Mrs. Udell is the editor of the clever monthly publication *Stylus,* and wherever it reaches and among all women she is known, her splendid talents are admired. Personally, Mrs. Udell comes near to Stanley Waterloo's description of the heroine of his story *A Man and a Woman,* whom he calls "a little brown streak." She is slight and a brunette, and her dark hair, brushed straight back, shows a broad and thoughtful brow. Though the black glasses, in hiding her misfortune, make a blur upon an interesting and attractive countenance, what is lost in expression for lack of eyes is in a great measure supplied by a wonderfully mobile mouth.

Mrs. Udell's subject last night was "Our Literary Idols," and she was an iconoclast among the chalk and plaster-of-paris images the "general reader" has set up. She used a

44 Published as an unsigned article in the *Freeport Daily Democrat,* Feb. 12, 1897.

cudgel of faint praise effectively on the heads of popular writers but sang the praises of the decadents. A woman of broad culture and wide reading, her criticisms were not the gibes of the phillistine, but a refined sarcasm emanating from a keen and superior mind.

Among the writers of recent years Mrs. Udell touched in her lecture was the once famous but now almost forgotten Marie Bashkirtseff. "In that wild journal of hers," she said, "Marie makes herself into her own heroine, an in her longing for notoriety she tells us everything about herself, to the minutest detail, and sometimes to the weariness of the reader. Can we not see her perfervid imagination, and morbid nature, that sensitiveness to criticism but seeking after notoriety, the picture of modern art?

"Recently there has been a new departure, what Max Nordau, and others, catching the word from him, has called the 'decadence.' The question is, what is a decadent? But if you ask it none will answer. Philosophically considered, there are two branches of them, one being the impressionist, the other the symbolist. The most striking figure of the impressionists is perhaps the French poet Milarmes,[45] with his contempt for the world so great one wonders if it is sincere. He unquestionably has genius, and his aim has been to create a new literature, but though night after night he has captured the fancy of the best young poets of Paris, he has contributed to literature but a few fragments of prose and verse.

"Other striking recent examples of the decadents are Paul Verlaine, the Frenchman, who writes such exquisite verse, and the Belgian dramatist, Maurice Maeterlinck. The best evidence of Maeterlincks' work is given in a little drama called *The Interior*. This figure of the night, this spirit of the

45 "Mallarmé"

grave, has risen to more than European importance, and is next after Ibsen, to whom he is strangely contasted, the great contemporary poet. He is to Belgian literature what Poe was to American.

"These flowers of an exotic fancy do not find a warm welcome in the American literary garden. We do not like dreamers. We are optimists and worshippers of the practical, which hurts our appreciation, so we have gracefulness of verse but little of the perfume of pure poetry."

Mrs. Udell said Riley's poems of nature bear the stamp of genuineness and eulogized the late Eugene Field highly. Among other contemporary poets, she mentioned as those "who are an echo of the decadents" Bliss Carman, Stephen Crane, and William Winter, reciting a poem of the latter, and also one each of Riley and Field, very gracefully.

"In humor," she continued, "American literature has made its best strides, yet there we have limitations, and the best writers direct all their shafts against innovations. We Americans are peculiar. We want our portraits painted but want all objectionable features left out. Two recent novels are striking departures: *The Damnation of Theron Ware* by Harold Frederick and *The Red Badge of Courage* by Stephen Crane. If those authors fulfill the promise of those two books, we may expect great things from them."

She gave Mr. Howells a setting-down as a "narrator of incidents without point. It is unquestionably realism. It is like going into society, only in the latter, can we avoid the bores, while in Mr. Howells' books, we find nothing else. Yet we call him our greatest American writer.

"Every one of the greatest European novelists," she went on, "has been called upon to answer the charge of immorality: Tolstoy, Zola, Hardy, Du Maurier, and even Grant Allen.

There is one notable exception, Madam Sarah Grand. If you want to read a book perfectly free from a hint of anything improper, or entertaining or interesting as well, go through *The Heavenly Twins*. We really wonder if the mass of readers have more virtues now or are the rest of us more corrupt than in the days of Hawthorne and Eliot. One thing that writers have to face is that relic of the seventh century, the conservatorship of letters. First are the critics—each secure in his own infallibility but each differing from the other, and then the followers of Anthony Comstock and that class of ladies who discharge for literature his functions in the court room but who never fail to read what they 'condemn,' perhaps to be better advised if it is fit for their husbands' and sons' reading. Anything that contains a passage their youngest daughter may not read is condemned. The truth is that literature is but a mirror that reflects life, and you might as well smash your pier glass[46] for reflecting the wrinkles of advancing age as to condemn artists for showing the wrinkles of Mrs. Grundy's[47] ancient face."

In conclusion, Mrs. Udell commented briefly on two books by Hall Caine and gave a review of contemporary French writers and literature.

46 A mirror hung between two windows.

47 A somewhat dated reference to someone who is extremely conventional and sometimes tyrannical, resistant to the new or unorthodox.

IN BEHALF OF THE EDUCATED BLIND

To the Editor of *The Republican*.

Sir: —In the *Democrat* of July 14 appears an unsigned article under the following misleading headlines: "Work of Blindman, Deprived of Sight by Accident. He Supports Family." The article refers to a man deprived of sight who has been selling pencils in the streets of Waterbury. The man has called attention to his infirmity by a placard on his sleeve bearing the word "Blind."

In behalf of the entire class of educated blind, and in accord with all experienced educators of the sightless, I beg to submit a respectful but earnest protest against the sentiment which the article in question contains. It is true, as the writer contends, that "A human being deprived of his sight who has the courage to tramp the country year in and year out, secure money in an honest way, and send it home to a wife who puts it to good use deserves to be encouraged." Legitimate salesmanship is undoubtedly a field in which the blind man may profitably engage. In that field, he may, and sometimes does, successfully compete with the seeing. He deserves all possible encouragement in this or in any other effort which he may make to achieve independence for himself and for his family, and the best service which society can render him will be to remove all obstacles from his path.

There are several ways in which a man or woman who cannot see may earn an honest living. There are trades such as broom-making, chair-seating, etc. at which they may work. The best of these is piano-tuning. There is a place for the blind man in several professions in music, in literature, in politics and in law. The highest success has even been attained by a few in medicine. What the educated blind ask of society is that their blindness shall not debar them from receiving whatever recognition their merit deserves. There is no reason why one of them may not be a first-class salesman, but there is no self-respecting and intelligent member of this class who does not resent the pauperizing kind of pity which recommends public or private begging to them as a means of subsistence. They contend that all placards such as the one used by this pretended seller of pencils place the user outside the category of salesmen and in that of beggars. They further maintain that any man or woman who obtains money by exploiting this infirmity not only degrades himself or herself but discredits thousands of citizens who, denied the use of one faculty, yet strive with honest pride to prove to the world that they are not inferior beings.

LILLIAN H. UDELL
Waterbury, July 16

Has Socialism a literature? This word "literature" is obviously not meant to be used here as a synonym for printed matter, as we speak of the literature of an anti-tuberculosis campaign or a vice crusade. One regrets the poverty of language which forces us to employ one and the same noun in describing the tragedy of an Aeschylus or an Ibsen and the report of a garbage inspector. Socialism has its men of science like Enrico Ferri, its philosophers like Dietzgen, its economists like Marx and Engels, its scholars like Kautsky and Ward, its men of action like Bebel, Haywood, and Debs.

In the present inquiry, we refer to the art by which noble thought finds adequate expression on the printed page, the medium through which aesthetic or heroic emotion becomes articulate for our own and succeeding generations.

For existence, even our present existence under the wage system has its aesthetic and heroic phases. None of us should forget that, least of all the pioneers in a revolutionary movement. Granted that the philosophers of the eighteenth century did not take the Bastile or achieve the cataclysm of '93, none the less, their work stands as the best inheritance of their time; none the less, their writings form the source of highest inspiration for their spiritual descendants of the twentieth century. What we of today are striving for is not merely physical well-being, nor even physical well-being plus a most intimate and accurate knowledge of our descent from the amoeba and our kinship with the chimpanzee. Does the Socialist movement as at present constituted afford us those elements of poetry and eloquence which nerve the spirit for the great act of rebellion which must precede the bringing in of a better order of things?

One recalls Oscar Wilde's *Soul of Man Under Socialism* and William Morris' *News from Nowhere*. These two master artists have, however, given us pictures of society in its ultimate perfection. Their prophecy is derived less from science than from faith. Mr. Shaw has treated current problems with a lucidity and brilliancy unsurpassed by any contemporary writer. But his appeal is never to the deeper emotions of his readers.

These thoughts occurred to me as I laid down a little volume entitled *Revolutionary Essays in Socialist Faith and Fancy*,[48] by Peter E. Burrowes.

I cannot claim for this author a very high place among literateurs, yet in his best moments, he is reminiscent of Carlyle, of Whitman, and, curiously enough, of Friedrich Nietzsche.

At his worst, he is mystical even to the point of becoming unintelligible. There is much in these essays that could have been omitted. Yet the reader who can enter into the mood in which the work is conceived will find himself abundantly repaid for the effort. There is throughout all these reflections a fine enthusiasm which acts upon one as a tonic. There are moments of passionate eloquence, almost of poetry. There is little that is dull. One feels that the man who penned them had the temperament of a poet. He is religious, but his religion is of this world. He writes,

> Oh, he is a very present, very near and dear God—the God whose new name I whisper to thee, Socialism. And as you think of the glistening morning thoughts, wherewith so often he has coronat-

48 Published by Charles H. Kerr & Company, Chicago, cloth, $1.00, postpaid.

> ed your brow, that crown of yours, which is in the thought world as a rich rose giving out of its folds delightful particles of fragrantly blessed fancies you know nevermore aught of the terrible nearness of God. He is no longer that awful live eye which the priests pulled out of a socket and set staring at you from the altar, staring in among your poor little heart thoughts, to shrivel you up with a horrible fear of God and make you slaves. The God of humanity is so sweetly near, and you so sweetly fearless of his nearness are, that you would if you could, let him into your bosom's heart to stay among the red pulses.

Yet this dreamer is far indeed from holding the point of view of the Christian Socialist. He is never more vehement, and perhaps never clearer in his utterance, than in his attack upon organized religion:

> There is no vision that ever came to man so unconquerably true as the Socialist perception that the church in every nation is but the voice of the economic ascendant. In America, many are puzzled to see mercantile Protestanism and mercantile infidelity flirting so incontinently with Rome. The daily press, which is indubitably run and written by trade and for trade only, cannot nevertheless conceal, and cannot hold back the daily interest of its proprietors in the prosperity and doings of that venerable hypnotist, the approved handmaiden and willing paramour of all despotism, the Roman Catholic Church. And let it be known that she deserves their confidence and affection, for she has never yet offi-

> cially betrayed any property class, and indeed cannot, for every cell and tissue of her canons, doctrines, and practices was formed in the bowels of riches for its own defense and comfort against the sinners who must work and who do not work enough.

And later,

> I do not single out Rome by name in order to separate her dishonorably from the other churches of the world. Her own claim that in Western lands she is the mother church is sound; she is older and wiser in the police business than her Protestant progeny, who though a bit naughty in the past, are filially imitative. It was but a minor property quarrel that separated them, the major property interest of uniting against Socialism will soon bring them all together again. Hence the billing and cooing between their eminences in the press and the priesthood.

The so-called progressive movement in modern capitalist politics will find here little encouragement:

> The reform tinker, who has no higher aim in politics than to mend the passing pots, we do not endorse. He shall pass through life mending pots, and shall leave the world with yet more pots to mend than he found there when he came.

We are to have no illusion concerning the depth of our slavery to those who own the tools of production:

> This parasite class, according to the observed law prevailing in all ages, having obtained control of the economic needs and forces of their time, clothe themselves with authority, and gird themselves with the powers of the state. They therefore can supplement the privation by exclusion from the means of living. They can also add positive suffering to the negative misery: they can beat you by all the rods of law into their laboratories; they can entangle your feet in every step you make for freedom; they can not only use the guns of the state against you but they can force you to use them against yourself; they can by possessing all the archives, know how much it is costing you to live, and can, as private employers, cut your wages down to that. From the signal boxes of the state they know your incoming and outgoing. They can control your mind; they can go behind you, and before/and float over you, and build military tunnels under your feet with your own hands. You cannot be emancipated while that class is in control and they can afford to let you play at all kinds of radical discontent as long as you leave them where they are.

And, oh, the contempt he pours upon the middle class:

> The middle class man is the negative, empty space between two facts, he is nothing—not even a hypocrite. He has no role to play anywhere in any great world. No great social movement is for him who is but a soaker, maintaining himself by keeping on the moister side of everything.

That which is of value in these essays is a certain power, born of earnest conviction, which meets Tolstoy's test of art, *viz.*, that the emotion of the writer is communicated to those who read. They are not literature, it is true, but they deserve to be read.

Into every generation are born certain personalities that have the gift of attracting vast multitudes within their orbit, dominating them, animating them with a single purpose, directing them to a common goal. There are other personalities more richly gifted, of more extended vision, who nevertheless live and die unknown to the greater number of their contemporaries. Aristocrats of the mind, these latter disdain to practice the arts by which popularity is gained and held. They attract but do not seek to dominate. They persuade but never command. Their passion is without hysteria; their moral indignation is without personal rancor. They cherish ideals but harbor no illusions. They will gladly surrender life itself for an idea, but they will not shriek for it. Our popular leaders are not seldom led by those who seem to follow. These others advance alone. If they are followed, it is without their solicitation. To say that the individualist writer and lecturer whose collected writings are now before us was such a personality may seem exaggerated praise. If so, I have no apology to offer. I only ask that until you have read the lectures, poems, stories, and sketches which this book contains, you will suspend judgment.

Voltairine de Cleyre belonged to the school of thinkers that has suffered most from the misrepresentations and misunderstanding of the unthinking crowd, the school which numbers among its adherents men like Stirner, Ibsen, and—in some aspects of his teaching—Nietzsche, the school that sees hope of social regeneration only in the sovereignty of the individual and the total abolition of the state. She belonged to it because she was at once logician and poet, with a temperament abnormally rebellious against tyranny and an imagination abnormally responsive to every form of suffering.

It has often been remarked that anarchism takes root most readily in those minds that have endured most oppression. Thus Russia, the home of absolute political despotism, is also the birthplace of Bakunin, Hertzen, Kropotkin, and Tolstoy. In America, where what Mencken calls "the new puritanism" operates more oppressively than political government, it is in behalf of sex freedom that most frequent and vehement protest is heard.

In the case of Voltairine de Cleyre, this reaction declared itself neither because of political nor of sexual restraint. It came about in the realm of religion. It began from the moment when, at the age of twelve, the sensitive, gifted girl was placed in the hands of a Roman Catholic sisterhood, presumably that her education might be safe. For four years, the young Voltairine lived at the convent of Our Lady of Lake Huron at Sarnia, Ontario, heartsick with loneliness, writhing under the padded yoke of conventual discipline, gathering within her soul that flame which was never destined to be quenched save in death. Out of that experience, she came with a mind wholly emancipated from the dogmas of religion. Not long afterward, she entered upon what promised to be a brilliant career as a secularist lecturer.

That a nature like hers would long confine itself to labor in the barren field of theological controversy was not to have been expected. She was too vital, too human. It is possible that the delicacy of her own health intensified her sense of the world's pain. Her sympathies are not alone of the intellect but of the nerves. One feels the nerve torture of an imaginative and poetic invalid in her confession of the reasons which had drawn her to adopt the anarchist propaganda. She pictures herself as standing upon a mighty hill, from which she writes,

> I saw the roofs of the workshops of the little world. I saw the machines, the things that men had made to ease their burden, the wonderful things, the iron genii; I saw them set their iron teeth in the living flesh of the men who made them; I saw the maimed and crumpled stumps of men go limping away into the night that engulfs the poor, perhaps to be thrown up in the flotsam and jetsam of beggary for a time, perhaps to suicide in some dim corner where the black surge throws its slime. I saw the rose fire of the furnace shining on the blanched face of the man who tended it, and knew surely, as I knew anything in life, that never would a free man feed his blood to the fire like that.
>
> I saw swart bodies, all mangled and crushed, borne from the mouths of the mines to be stowed away in a grave hardly less narrow and dark than that in which the living form had crouched ten, twelve, fourteen hours a day, and I knew that in order that I might be warm—I and you, and those others who never do any dirty work—those men had slaved away in those black graves and been crushed to death at last.
>
> I saw beside city streets great heaps of horrible-colored earth, and down at the bottom of the trench from which it was thrown, so far down that nothing else was visible, bright gleaming eyes, like a wild animal hunted into its hole. And I knew that free men never chose to labor there, with pick and shovel, in that foul, sewage-soaked earth, in that

narrow trench, in that deadly sewer gas, ten, eight, even six hours a day. Only slaves would do it.

I saw deep down in the hull of the ocean liner the men who shoveled the coal—burned and seared like paper before the grate, and I knew that "the record" of the beautiful monster, and the pleasure of the ladies who laughed on the deck, were paid for with those withered bodies and souls. I saw the scavenger carts go up and down, drawn by sad brutes and driven by sadder ones; for never a man, a man in full possession of his selfhood, would freely choose to spend all his days in the nauseating stench that forces him to swill alcohol to neutralize it. And I saw in the lead works how men were poisoned, and in the sugar refineries how they went insane, and in the factories how they lost their decency, and in the stores how they learned to lie, and I knew it was slavery made them do all this.

And against such slavery, this young Amazon of the spirit (for at this time, 1887, she was only twenty-one) declared a life-long warfare. In so doing, she separated herself from those who would otherwise have been her natural allies and cut off those opportunities for worldly success which must, in the ordinary course of things, have come to her.

Finding the cause of economic slavery not in capitalism, as do the socialists, but in the government of man by man, through which capitalism is made possible, she was isolated still further from her contemporaries. Hence the obscurity in which her life was passed. Hence the fact that until her death in 1912, she lived quietly, teaching English to the newly arrived immigrant, scattering about her the treasure of a richly-stored mind as freely as the south wind scatters the perfume it has gathered from the garden in its path. If she had lived nearer to the plane of the generally accepted culture, Voltairine de Cleyre might have gained a recognized place among the foremost women of her time.

As it was, she gave us in her lectures, now for the first time offered to the public, the most comprehensive exposition of philosophical anarchism that has appeared since the days of Proudhon and Stirner.

BOOK REVIEWS FROM THE INTERNATIONAL SOCIALIST REVIEW

FROM VOL. VI, NO. 3, SEPTEMBER 1905

***My Little Book of Prayer* by Muriel Strofe, 2nd Edition. The Open Court Publishing Co., Chicago, Ill.**

Just why this title should have been chosen is not apparent. It is true that the author's attitude is often one of prayer, but it is quite as often one of direct affirmation. What we have here is really a collection of aphorisms and emotional utterances, unrelated to one another except in so far as they are the expressions of a single more or less constant mood.

One does not look for any distinct philosophy in a book of this character, and one does not find it here. Obviously, the writer is an individualist, but individualism such as hers, which seeks for itself a new path not because the paths trodden by others have been found undesirable but merely to taste the exhilaration of novelty, such individualism springs rather from temperament than from reasoned conviction.

The theology of the book seems considerably mixed, but so is most theology.

Here and there, we find tiny fragments of, shall we say, prose, poetry, or poetic prose.

These show, indeed, no great degree of original talent, but they are graceful both in thought and imagery. The following is illustrative:

> Better than tiaras—the diadem of freedom.
> Better than broad acres—a garland of heartsease.
> Better than mines of gold—a mint of dreams.
> Better than bars of silver—the silver of a laugh.
> Better than strings of pearls—the crystal of a tear.
> Better than bands of choristers—a lute in the soul.

From Vol. VI, No. 6, December 1905

***Germs of Mind in Plants* by R. H. Francé. Translated by A. M. Simons. Charles H. Kerr & Co., 1905, cloth, 147 pp., 50c.**

The history of modern scientific knowledge is the history of our advance toward a monistic conception of the universe. In the Cartesian philosophy, a sharp division was conceived between man and the lower animals, the latter figuring as mere automata, devoid of sensation. Though the progress of science quickly dispelled that illusion, still more than two centuries had to pass before men could discern all the links which make the unbroken chain of organic life. During that period, no serious investigator dreamed of ascribing to the vegetable kingdom any power of feeling or of initiative. With the advent of the new botany, all this was changed. Plants were seen to be endowed with sensation which differs only in degree from that possessed by their superiors in the scale of development, even by man himself. In the suggestive and poetic nature study now before us, we see a picture of mind stuff in the making. We see trees and flowers taking rest and nourishment, defending themselves against injury, and seeking spontaneously those conditions most favorable to their growth. We see indications of the actual presence of the senses of smell and taste among them. We observe their sensitiveness to temperature, to the force of gravity, to a multitude of stimuli, many of which are far too delicate for human perception. What then do we learn from revelations like this? Simply the underlying oneness of all life. What do we infer? Simply the unity of the universe. The author does not attempt more than an introduction to this subject, neither does he claim for himself any special originality, but he views nature with the eyes of a man of science and tells us of his visions in the language of a poet. A philosopher he is not, and perhaps it is just the poetic quality of his mind which colors and confuses his philosophical conceptions. For instance, this little treatise is beyond question a document in support of monism, and the author recognizes the tendency of his own teaching. Nevertheless, on more than one occasion, we find him losing sight of his central truth, as in the following passage:

> I have often thought that the peculiar riddle of life consisted in just this—how an apparently all powerful creativeness can be united to a scheme of physical forces. Perhaps the wisdom of Empedocles offers the true solution, and there is an unconfined spirit in everything, which can only gradually free itself from the bonds of matter—most of all in us, less in the animals, and still less in the plants, and becoming in its lowest manifestation only perceptible, as an eternal causal relation, in dead matter itself. This poetical figure is perhaps the best description of the reality.

We agree with France that this is a poetic figure, but we cannot agree with him that it stands for reality. "Unconfined spirit" is unconceivable since we only know spirit as it exists within the confines of material substance, and as for the phrase "dead matter," it means nothing since not a particle of matter exists destitute of the power of initiative, destitute of the potentiality of life. Evidently, too, France still cherishes a belief in Kant's "thing in itself." On this point, however, the translator's note is a sufficient reply.

From Vol. VI, No. 8, February 1906

***The End of the World* by Dr. M. Wilhelm Meyer, translated by Margaret Wagner, Chas. H. Kerr & Co., Chicago.**

> We seem to exist in a hazardous time,
> Driftin' along here through space;

Nobody knows just when we begun
Or how fur we've gone in the race.
Scientists argy we're shot from the sun,
While others we're going right back,
An' some say we've allers been here more or less,
An' seem to establish the fact
O' course 'at's' somepin' 'at nobody knows,
As far as I've read or cun see;
An' them as does know all about the hull scheme,
Why, none of 'em never agree.

These homely but genial verses of Ben King were suggested to me by Dr. Meyer's interesting essay entitled "The End of the World." It is not that there is anything flippant or superficial in the author's treatment of his subject, but there is a contagious cheerfulness about his manner of reviewing the possibilities of sudden or slow world dissolution which almost provokes a smile. It is curious to observe the effect produced by the same data upon men of differing temperaments. Mr. W. H. Mallock contemplates the extinction of the human race and becomes a profound pessimist. Dr. Meyer views the entire panorama of ceaseless change throughout the universe and finds in it only a confirmation of his optimism. Nature, according to him, destroys only to upbuild in grander style. This seems to me to be a far-reaching conclusion, not justified by our present imperfect knowledge of cosmic phenomena. Is it not more true to the facts in the case to conceive of the cosmos as in a state of constant equilibrium, in which the forces that make for evolution and dissolution balance each other? Still, for us, it remains also true that our planet has not passed beyond the stage of earliest youth. Our author suggests this and the further probability that millions of years must pass before "the terrible coldness of icy space well enwrap the earth." The book is a study of cosmic decay in which familiar facts are presented in a style certain to prove attractive to the average reader interested in such themes.

FROM VOL. VII, NO. 4, OCTOBER 1906

***Life and Death, A Study In Biology* by Dr. E. Teichmann. Translated by A. M. Simons.**

> "Samuel speaks: 'Science will not suffice. Sooner or later, you will end by coming to your knees.'
> Goetze: 'Before what?'
> Samuel: 'Before the darkness.'
>
> —Villiers De L'Isle Adam.

This bit of dialogue from a celebrated French play reflects the mental attitude to which most imaginative men come when they desert fact for speculation and seek to compass in thought the final causes of things.

It is the attitude of Omar in the tenth as of Herbert Spencer in the nineteenth century. It is hinted at in the latest utterances of Prof. Ernest Haeckel and in the earliest lispings of Greek philosophy. We are not surprised, therefore, to find this state of mind reflected in the essay before us. But to those who feel with the translator that this view savors too much of theology, it may be urged that certainly nowhere else in the book is there any indication of theological bias. On the contrary, the author's treatment of his subject seems to us scientific from beginning to end.

We have here a study of life phenomena as they are revealed in the simplest organisms. Experiment after experiment is brought before us, each so selected as to show us some forward step taken in organic evolution, all so graphically described that the reader's attention is never for an instant taxed to the point of weariness. Indeed, we can say of this little volume what we are seldom able to predicate of similar studies, that it manages to be most entertaining without losing its value from the standpoint of science.

We are shown how life appears, how it reproduces itself; we view the transmission of qualities from parent to offspring by means of the division of nucleal substance. We are carried through a discussion of the origin of life without, however, receiving any answer to our question, "Whence have we come?" Last and most interesting of all is the inquiry into the subject of death. What Dr. Teichmann says on this point is full of an unexpected encouragement to those sensitive spirits to whom death makes life a tragedy. One takes leave of this essayist with the same mingling of regret and satisfaction which one feels after an evening spent with a helpful and inspiring friend.

FROM VOL. XV, NO. 4, OCTOBER 1914

Songs of Rebellion by Adolf Wolff. New York: Alfred and Chas. Boni. $1.00.

Goethe has said that no real circumstance is unpoetical so long as the poet knows how to use it. Whether the author of these verses has known how to use the materials he has chosen for his art is a matter whose decision will rest, in the last analysis, upon the individual taste of the reader. But so, in fact, does all criticism.

Assuredly, he maintains towards the universe and toward all of its phenomena the attitude of a poet. Assuredly, too, he is daring, nothing if not daring. That some of his pieces display a genuine, if modest, gift of lyricism cannot, I think, be denied. At the risk of being called a Philistine, I hazard the belief that with a little more attention to the requirements of rhyme and rhythm, the entire level of the performance would have been distinctly raised.

I especially liked the lines beginning "I thought you dead, I thought you dead to me", liked them, that is, because they sing themselves.

I confidently believe that by the unsparing application of self-criticism, by holding no law higher than the promptings of his own talent—save the law of beauty itself—and by avoiding such great, but for him dangerous models as Walt Whitman this young writer will eventually become in form what he already is in spirit—a true poet.

The Social Significance of the Modern Drama by Emma Goldman.

In a dynamic age like ours it is quite natural that literary art should achieve its supreme expression in the drama, that is to say, in the literature of action. At a time when thinking men everywhere are busied in the great task of transvaluation, it is inevitable that that drama shall declare war against ancient and generally accepted values. One is amused to observe the zeal which the clergymen and the conventional critic display: the one in depreciating the merit of modern plays, the other in obscuring under the dust of technical discussion their real significance.

Not the least important service which Emma Goldman has rendered us in these lectures has been to uncover the revolutionary message of the contemporary drama so that he who runs may read.

It may be that her interpretations differ in some instances from those which the authors of these plays would have given. In one case, that of *Damaged Goods*, M. Brieux's obvious teaching on the subject of marriage seems to have been passed over in silence. Indeed, this playwright is not more revolutionary than are many of the participants in our state and national conferences of charities and corrections. To say this, however, is not to detract in any way from the merit of Miss Goldman's book as an eloquent and stimulating introduction to a study which no socialist of whatever school can afford to neglect.

Henry Demarest Lloyd: A Biography **by Caro Lloyd. New York: G. P. Putnams Sons. $5.00.**

Evolution and revolution—progress has been attained in both ways: the irresistible advance through long and painful periods of times and the equally irresistible cataclysms brought about by sudden and imperious necessity, which respects no theories about progress, no matter how reasonable or scientific they may seem. The events of the world may be symbolized in its Napoleons and its Adam Smiths.

The way in which we as individuals react to the pain of the world can only be explained by that elusive word—temperament. The present biography gives an interesting example of the workings of a mind disciplined in the scientific-evolutionary school.

Lloyd was a man keenly sensitive to the sufferings of his fellow men. Yet throughout his long and useful life—1847–1903—we see the temperament of an earnest student, a student who is firmly convinced that the tragedy of the world can gradually be diminished by carefully thought-out scientific remedies, peacefully applied. We see him, note book in hand, studying all the symptoms of social disease, analyzing, classifying, arranging, re-arranging, piling fact upon fact, that he might frame an argument strong enough to touch all men by sheer force of logic. He thus accumulated enough adverse data regarding the Standard Oil Company to dissolve seventeen "wicked" corporations, yet somehow the Standard Oil Company refused to disappear. Why? Because Lloyd, in all his attacks upon the strongholds of tyranny, was not the spokesman for a militant working class conscious of its burdens and conscious of its power. He remained but a detached and generous observer.

 NOTICES FROM THE DAY BOOK 

The following items are from the Chicago proletariat daily newspaper *The Day Book* between March 1915 and December 1916.

MONDAY, MARCH 8, 1915

Mrs. Udell will speak before Modern Self Educational League tonight at Maxwell Settlement, 1214 S. Clinton. Subject: "Young Generation and Revolution."

MONDAY, APRIL 26, 1915

Mrs. Udell will address Modern Self Educational League at Maxwell Settlement, 1214 Clinton, tonight.

FRIDAY, AUGUST 6, 1915

Modern education from the anarchistic standpoint will be the subject of a lecture by Mrs. Udell at I.W.W. hall, 644 W. 12th st., tonight.

MONDAY, APRIL 17, 1916

Lillian Hiller Udell to begin series of four Tues. evening studies of renaissance in poetry and drama for Green Room Circle, Arlington Hotel, Tues., 8 p.m. Ibsen first study.

TUESDAY, MAY 16, 1916

Lecture by Lillian Hiller Udell at 19 W. Pearson tonight. Irish literary movement and plays of Yeats, Synge and Lady Gregory will be discussed.

TUESDAY, MAY 18, 1916

Lillian Hillier Udell, who because of illness was unable to give her lecture, "Irish Movement in Poetry and Drama,"

19 W. Pearson, Tues. night, will deliver the lecture there, 8:30 p.m., Thurs.

MONDAY JUNE 12, 1916

Lillian Hiller Udell, will lecture 19 W. Pearson, Tues. night, "Dostoiffsky and Turgeniev."

MONDAY, JUNE 19, 1916

Memorial meeting, fourth anniversary Voltairine de Cleyre, Bowen Hall, Hull House, Tues., 8 p. m. Addresses by Lillian Hiller Udell, E. C. Wentworth, J. Abrams, A. T. Tobinson, L. Blume, Honore Jaxon and others.

MONDAY, JULY 10, 1916

"Feminism in Literature," lecture by Lillian H. Udell, 19 W. Pearson, Tuesday night.

TUESDAY, JULY 25, 1916

Lilian Hiller Udell will lecture at 19 W. Pearson tonight: "Maeterlinck and Verhaeren."

MONDAY, AUGUST 7, 1916

Lillian Hiller Udell lectures "Belgian Renaissance in Literature," Liberty hall, 2941 Indiana av., Tuesday night.

MONDAY, AUGUST 21, 1916

Lillian Hiller Udell lectures, Tues. night, Liberty Hall, 2941 Indiana av.: "Henrik Ibsen as a Poet."

TUESDAY, SEPTEMBER 6, 1916

Lillian Hiller Udell will lecture on Henrik Ibsen's *Brand* at Liberty Hall, 2941 Indiana av., tonight.

Tuesday, September 19, 1916

Lillian Hiller Udell will lecture von Ibsen's "Peer Gynt" at Liberty Hall, 2941 Indiana av., tonight.

Wednesday, October 11, 1916

Society of Anthropology, 2:30 p. m., Sun., Corinthian Hall, Masonic Temple. "Francis Fareer's System of Education."[49] Lillian Hiller Udell.

Monday, November 6, 1916

Lillian Hiller Udell will deliver first of four lectures on "Spirit of Irish Literature" at Liberty Hall tonight.

Monday, November 20, 1916

Lillian Hiller Udell will lecture on, "Poet Patriots of Ireland" tonight at Liberty Hall, 2941 Indiana av. Discussion.

Monday, December 4, 1916

Lillian Hiller Udell will lecture at Liberty Hall, 2941 Indiana av., Wed., Dec. 6, instead of 7th, as announced. Subject: "Revival of Irish Poetry."

49 The name is spelled "Farrer" in the source, but this is certainly a reference to "François Marie Charles Fourier", commonly "Charles Fourier."

BOOK SALE

20 to 50 Per Cent. Off on
RADICAL BOOKS

Economics

Sociology

History

Fiction

Poetry

Drama

NEW BARGAINS ADDED DAILY
THROUGH FEBRUARY

Hours 1 P. M. to 10 P.M. Daily & Sunday

RADICAL BOOK SHOP

Superior 9168 826 N. Clark St.

▲ Advetisement from *The New Majority*, Vol.7, No.6, Feb. 11th, 1922. Of note is the addition of a phone number.

INDEX

D

E

F

G

H

I

J

K

L

M

N

O

P

Q

U

V

W

Y

Z

Made in the USA
Middletown, DE
20 April 2023